KV-194-217

THE JUDITH BERRISFORD BOOK OF BASIC PONY CARE

An essential guide for pony lovers and pony owners.

The Judith Berrisford Book of Basic Pony Care has been written with the insight of many years of practical experience of pony handling – offering expert and responsible advice for young owners. The information included covers numerous points not to be found in other books: buying a suitable pony, joining a pony club, grooming for shows, correct feeding, attending to ailments, and safety in traffic.

The complete guide to pony care.

About the author

Judith Berrisford is famous for her best-selling, very readable pony stories which combine excitement and adventure with plenty of fascinating pony lore and horsy background. She lives with her husband by the sea, where they both enjoy outdoor interests – walking, swimming, bird-watching, gardening, and, of course, horses and ponies.

Stories by Judith Berrisford published by Knight Books are:
Pippa's Mystery Horse
Pippa and the Midnight Ponies

The Judith Berrisford Book of Basic Pony Care

KNIGHT BOOKS
Hodder and Stoughton

This book is affectionately dedicated to
three super pony-wise people,
Victoria, William and Sally Jagger.

Copyright © 1987 Judith M. Berrisford
Illustrations copyright © Hodder & Stoughton Ltd. 1987

First published by Knight Books 1987

British Library C.I.P.

Berrisford, Judith M.
The Judith Berrisford book of basic
pony care.
1. Ponies – Juvenile literature
I. Title
636.1'6   SF315

ISBN 0-340-40859-6

Printed and bound in Great Britain for
Hodder and Stoughton Paperbacks, a
division of Hodder and Stoughton Ltd.,
Mill Road, Dunton Green, Sevenoaks,
Kent (Editorial Office: 47 Bedford
Square, London WC1B 3DP) by
Richard Clay Ltd., Bungay, Suffolk
Photoset by Rowland Phototypesetting Ltd.,
Bury St Edmunds, Suffolk.

CONTENTS

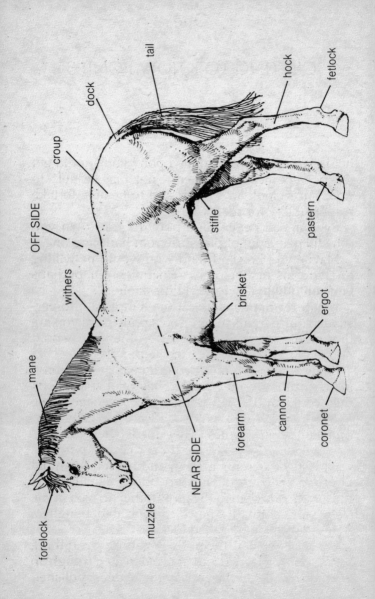

tail
dock
croup
hock
fetlock
OFF SIDE
stifle
withers
pastern
mane
brisket
ergot
NEAR SIDE
forearm
forelock
cannon
muzzle
coronet

One

GETTING TO KNOW PONIES

Before you think of owning a pony you should get to know ponies really well – not just be able to ride, but to look after them and to be able to take responsibility for their well-being.

Even if you never get a pony of your own you can still gain a lot of pleasure from handling one.

Maybe you have a friend who would be willing to share his or her pony sometimes. Or perhaps you could help at a local riding stable.

Whatever happens, resist the temptation to persuade your parents to buy you a pony until you are thoroughly experienced. To do otherwise would not be fair to yourself – or to the pony!

Some time ago I met two girls who were pony-mad, or thought they were. They read every book they could find about ponies. They begged some old tack which they enjoyed cleaning. They day-dreamed about ponies. They made their parents' lives a misery by pestering them to buy a pony.

At last the parents gave in and moved to an old house in the country with a paddock. Finally came the exciting day when the girls' father arrived home from work with the news that he had bought a pony – a grey mare called Pickles.

The girls busied themselves getting everything ready. They cleaned out the old water trough in the field, made up the gaps in the hedges, polished up the ancient bridle and the saddle which needed re-stuffing.

At last Pickles arrived. The trailer bringing her turned up late at night because the car towing it had a breakdown on the way.

The girls were in bed and alseep and when they woke up next morning and looked out of the window there was the pony, *their* pony, grazing in the field. It was like magic.

Still in their pyjamas they dashed outside. They ran across the dew-wet grass to claim the pony – and that was where the magic stopped and reality began. Because although the sisters had read so much about ponies, talked about them, dreamed of nothing else, they had never even had a riding lesson. Worse still, they had never been really near a pony on the ground, never helped to brush or bridle a pony, never done more than offer a handful of grass over a fence.

So, when Pickles, who was in a strange field and feeling lonely, trotted inquistively over to them to make friends the girls lost their nerve and ran away, with what now seemed a quite large – and very puzzled – animal thundering after them.

The girls had made a bad start. They were now nervous of the pony and Pickles sensed it, which made her nervous and uneasy, too.

Luckily one of the neighbours was pony-wise and able to help. She looked after Pickles to begin with and gradually helped the sisters to gain confidence so that they could enjoy caring for their pony.

All was well that ended well, but it might not have done – and it need never have happened, if only the girls and their parents had spent some time really getting to know about ponies and becoming used to handling them before buying one.

Understanding ponies

Ponies are sensitive animals and easily startled. They do not see as well as we do and so are apt to be taken by surprise. A dozing pony might be frightened by anyone creeping up on him un-noticed.

Always speak a friendly word of greeting when you go up to a pony and be sure to approach him from the front or side. This is important because a startled pony might kick out with his hind legs. In any case you want your first encounter to be a happy experience for a pony and not an occasion for fright.

Although I am not a great believer in too many tit-bits, I do think it helps to give the pony some little treat when first you meet. Do not give sugar to which many ponies become addicted and then demanding about. Have in your pocket, as a reward for the pony allowing itself to be caught or when it has done something well, a crust of bread, a piece of toast, a Polo mint or two, or carrot or apple sliced lengthwise into thick fingers. Fruit and root-vegetables should never be cut into round pieces because a greedy pony might swallow them whole and choke.

Making friends

When you first approach a pony walk up to it slowly and in a friendly way. Speak to it quietly and give it an encouraging pat or scratch it gently on the neck or shoulder. Then offer it a tit-bit on the outstretched palm of your hand.

Avoid touching the pony's face or ears until it knows you well and has learned to trust you. Some shy ponies will flinch from a stranger patting them but will usually accept a gentle and sympathetic rub on the shoulder or neck.

Try to visit a pony several times in its field so that it can get to know you before you attempt to catch it. Ask to be allowed to give it a feed and stay talking quietly to the pony while it is eating. Remember, though, never attempt to pat or pet a pony while it is eating.

Spend as much time with your chosen pony as possible so that it doesn't come to associate you just with treats or with lessons. Let the pony get to know you as a friend.

At the same time try to understand the pony's moods. The best indicators of these are its ears. Whenever you approach a strange pony watch the ears.

A friendly, interested pony will prick its ears forward and look towards you. If the pony's ears are relaxed, neither back nor forward, it is probably dozing. As you approach and speak its name quietly the ears will prick in expectation of a pleasant encounter. If, however, a pony should ever lay its ears back flat at your approach, beware! The pony might be bad-tempered, having been mishandled in the past, or it might be feeling uncomfortable – perhaps with a touch of colic. This might especially be the case if the pony's eyes are showing a lot of white, or rolling. If this happens, do not attempt to go up to the pony by yourself but fetch some responsible and knowledgeable adult to have a look at it.

Catching a pony

Some ponies can be difficult to catch, so if your

parents are thinking of buying you a pony, ask them to make sure they buy one which is sold as easy to catch. Never chase a pony or try to corner it. Coax it to come to a call. Try to visit the field with a tit-bit at the same time each day. Then, while the pony is munching, slip a piece of rope round its neck and pat it gently or scratch its neck or shoulder while you talk to it encouragingly. Do this on each visit, whether you intend to catch the pony for a ride or not. After a little while even the shyest pony will begin to look forward to your visit and respond by coming up readily when you appear.

Some pony owners use a leather head-collar and turn the pony out in that, feeling that having something to grasp makes the animal easier to catch. This is not always a good idea. If a pony is loose in a field, the headcollar may get caught up on a branch when rubbing against a tree. Or the leather might catch on a strand of wire or a broken piece of wood in a fence. Worse still, the pony might get its shoe caught up in one of the straps while scratching its head with a hind foot. It is wiser to accustom a pony to come readily to you for a piece of bread and a pat, familiarising it at the same time with the feel of the rope round its neck so that it accepts a halter easily.

Leading in hand

In the show-ring, in the field, or when being led about a riding school a pony should be led from the left.

It is a good idea to practise leading the pony from either side. It is customary and correct on most occasions, and particularly in the show ring, to lead from the left, or the pony's 'near' side when you are standing beside it facing front.

However, when on the highway you should always place yourself between the pony and the traffic for safety's sake, as you will then have more control and the pony will be less likely to panic. In Britain ponies, like cars and bicycles, have to keep to the left-hand side of the road so this means placing yourself on the pony's right or 'off' side. You will then have to lead from the right.

When leading from the left or 'near' side, you should take the lead-rope in your right hand near the pony's muzzle, taking up the slack with your left so that there is no free end trailing near the animal's legs. Consequently, when leading from the right of 'off' side, you should hold the lead-rope near the muzzle in your left hand and take up the slack with your right.

Turning a pony into a field

Hastily turned out ponies, whose owners whip off the halter as soon as they are inside the field and send them off with a hearty slap, often become difficult to catch. Ponies are easily excited, and the habit of galloping off immediately they are freed becomes ingrained. The pony starts to associate the presence of its owner in the field with galloping away instead of with a tit-bit or being made much of and so there is trouble. They may then buck or kick out in their high spirits, striking you by mistake.

When your ride is over and you return your pony to its field, take things easily. Make it stand while you shut the gate. Lead it about twenty paces into the field. Turn yourself round to face the gate.

Give the pony a pat and talk to it for a few minutes, perhaps rewarding it with a piece of carrot or a crust for good behaviour on the ride. Then remove the halter. Pat and talk to the pony again and walk away quietly leaving it looking forward to your next visit.

Two

FIRST FIND A FIELD

Before you persuade your parents to buy you a pony you must think where it might practicably be kept.

You may be lucky and have a field or paddock adjacent to your house. Failing this, you will probably have to rent grazing, for ponies need a lot to eat.

It might be possible to arrange with a local riding school to keep your pony for you but this is usually expensive. It might be cheaper if you could undertake to look after the pony yourself on what is called a 'Do It Yourself' livery arrangement. This might work well provided the riding school was not too far from your home. Remember, though, that you would have to visit the pony at least once a day, rain or shine, whatever the weather, term-time or holidays, to check it over, see that it had water and – during the colder months – take it additional feed.

This arrangement would have the advantage that you would have knowledgeable help to hand and someone to act as stand-in should you be ill or prevented by some other emergency from seeing to your pony yourself.

Finding alternative grazing

Sometimes you will see grazing to rent offered in a local paper.

Or you could get your parents to advertise for a field or you might persuade a local farmer to rent you grazing. If you are lucky, you might be able to share with some other pony owner. So long as the ponies get to know each other and are friendly this is ideal. Ponies are always happier with a companion. It is often a form of unwitting cruelty to keep a pony alone. Cattle, a donkey, even a few sheep to share the grazing are to be preferred to the pony being alone.

However fine the field, a pony that is on its own for much of the day becomes bored and mopey. Or it may get into mischief and try to break out in search of company.

If you choose a donkey as companion for your pony make sure it is properly tested by a vet for lungworm which does not affect the donkey but causes a nasty cough in ponies (see *worms* in Chapter 8).

It helps, of course, if the field is near your house where the pony can see people coming and going and where some member of the household might go out and talk to it occasionally while you are at school. On the other hand, too many passers-by can be a nuisance.

A friend of mine had a pony, a strawberry roan, which was kept in a field near the local junior school. So many children made friends with the pony and gave it tit-bits that the pony grew too fat. What was worse, it started to make a nuisance of itself with its owner, badgering her for tit-bits all the time. Then it began to nip when constant treats were not forthcoming. In the end she put up a notice: Please Do Not Feed the Pony. She asked the headmistress to explain to the children that sweets and lumps of sugar were ruining the pony's temper

– if not its teeth – and agreed to take the pony to give rides at the school fête, if by then its manners had improved.

Other people can create trouble by interfering with one's pony in this way. Fortunately most people are well meaning and kind. Once the problem is explained to them and their help sought they are willing to co-operate.

The ideal field

What kind of grazing does your pony need? The field should offer some shelter from rain and wind and also from sun and flies. Failing a high hedge, shady trees, a good clump or thicket of gorse, you will need to provide an open-fronted shed – solid walls on three sides to keep off the worst of the rain and wind and the fourth side open so that the pony does not feel trapped. This is particularly necessary where two or three ponies are sharing the field because one of the ponies might be afraid of being kicked or bullied by the others and will not use the shed unless it can get out quickly.

Very often in winter time ponies seem not to be using their shed. You will see them standing out against a hedge that is giving them partial protection from the rain or sleet. But in summer when the flies are troublesome they will suddenly decide to use their shelter and be only too glad to get away from the midges.

Water

Water is essential. All ponies need a plentiful

supply of clean water. A field with a running stream and a good solid bottom is perfect. However a stream with a sandy bottom may be a source of trouble, as the pony in drinking may suck up grains of sand and get sand colic. A stagnant muddy pond will not do. Some farmers have piped water in their fields with troughs fitted with a ballcock so that the trough automatically fills with fresh water once the animals have drunk. Even this needs regular inspection to make sure that dirt or weeds are not either causing the trough to flood or preventing the flow of water.

The great majority of fields have no such arrangements. There may be a trough which you will have to fill by hand each day or you may have to provide your own container. Whatever you use will have to be solid and firmly based so that the pony cannot knock it over. Old baths will not do. Not only do they look sordid but they usually have sharp sides that can cut a pony's legs.

Only the other day I heard of a pony narrowly escaping serious injury through the use of one of these old baths. The pony was wearing a head-collar – again I think this inadvisable in the case of a pony at grass – and the headcollar caught on one of the taps. The pony reared, panicked and pulled back, dragging the bath after her and cutting her leg.

Luckily the owner was at hand and she was able to calm the pony and so prevent further disaster. She immediately removed the taps and had the bath boarded around the sides to prevent anything like it happening again.

The moral of this story is that if you *have* to use an old bath make sure that the taps are removed and that the sides are properly covered with wooden boards. Better still, if you can possibly afford it, buy a trough.

Remember that any permanent water receptacle must be thoroughly cleaned and scrubbed out several times a year.

Fencing

Any field you choose must be soundly fenced or hedged so as to keep the pony in. You do not want the bother of a straying pony which might endanger itself by getting into traffic, or cause nuisance and damage to other people by getting into crops or gardens. It will be your responsibility to keep the pony safely in its field.

So before you get your pony, thoroughly inspect the field, looking at all walls, hedges, fences and gates, and make sure there are no weak places through which an animal might push. Get someone to help you to make any such places good. It is no use just filling the gap with a piece of wire or brush wood. You need someone strong to knock in stakes, replace rails and make a really firm job. Ponies rub against any convenient post or stake, especially in spring or autumn when they are changing their coats. They will soon break a weak place down again.

It is always helpful to creosote any stakes in order to protect them from rot. The creosote also discourages ponies from eating them.

Wire fences can be dangerous because any loose strands might catch against a pony's legs or shoulders and cause a wound. Even worse, if the pony is rubbing its head or neck against the fence, loose wire might catch it in the eye and could blind it. Reject any grazing which is surrounded by barbed wire or else persuade the farmer to change it.

All fences and hedges should be inspected regularly. It goes almost without saying that the gate should be easy to open and shut. This is essential when you are leading the pony out or in. You must ensure also that there is a secure catch or latch. Some ponies become expert at pushing up the latch with their nose or pulling up a loop of wire with their teeth. The moral is never to use a wire loop to fasten a gate. Make sure there is a proper galvanised gate-hook that the pony cannot undo.

Some snags to look out for

These days, litter can be a real hazard. Try to inspect the field each day for bottles or tins on which the

pony might get cut, or for plastic bags which could be lethal should the animal get one over its head or chew it.

Look out for any holes in which the pony might twist a fetlock. These should be filled in with earth and trodden well down.

Watch out for any old dead branches or twigs sticking out at pony eye-level and get someone to saw them off close to the tree.

Cut down any thistles and dig up and remove any poisonous plants like deadly nightshade, the tall straggly ragwort with its yellow daisies, fox-gloves and horsetail. Yew trees can be dangerous to ponies and cattle and should be fenced off securely. Always remove any cut-down weeds, etc from the field. Cut ragwort is even more deadly than the growing plant.

Management of grazing

All droppings should be collected regularly. Your parents might be glad of these to manure the garden, or they can be bagged and sold to help pay for the pony's keep.

A pony cannot be kept in the same small field all the time. Land constantly used for grazing without a break gets horse-sick. Fields must be rested periodically and treated. Serious infestations of red worm can occur if fields are grazed for too long continuously.

If the field is large enough, an electric fence can be used to divide it. This will give one half the chance to recover and for the parasites to die off while the other half is being grazed.

Every pony needs at least an acre and a half of

grazing to itself. If an area of this size is kept in good condition the average pony should do well off it, provided it is given additional food during the winter and seasons when grass is poor (see Chapter Four). Of course if the field is being shared with other animals, allowance must also be made for their grazing, too.

The best guide to the quality of the grass is the condition of the pony. An animal that looks sleek, contented and reasonably plump is obviously getting enough nourishment. A pony that stands head and tail down, 'tucked up', and looks thin with a staring coat needs additional food.

Naturally the time of year affects the way the grass grows. In late spring and early summer grass will be rich. Too much grazing at that time of the year can be bad for a pony. This is the time to partition the field to give part of it a chance to recover. Alternatively you can fasten the pony in a stable or in its shelter during the daytime so that it cannot blow itself out on too much tempting grass. You might also allow a few cattle or sheep into the field to help to eat the grass.

For a pony to share a field with cattle is an ideal method of ensuring that the ranker, long grass is pulled off and that the field is kept sweet and evenly grazed. On their own, ponies are patchy grazers and this leads to an uneven, poor growth of grass.

An open-sided shelter can be turned into a temporary stable by the use of hurdles or poles to close off the open side. Should there be two or more ponies it would be necessary to partition the shelter so that each pony has its own section.

Ponies rapidly become bored. To give them haynets to pull at during the day would defeat the object of keeping them away from their grazing so that they don't become too fat. Boredom has to be overcome by other means. Toys in the shape of old motor tyres or straw-filled sacks suspended from the roof gives them something to bodge at and so distracts their attention. Plastic orangeade bottles filled with pebbles and hung from the roof will serve a similar purpose. A turnip with a hole bored through the middle and suspended on a string will give the pony something to nibble that does not contain enough food value to do any harm.

You will need advice to help you make the best of your field. A nearby farmer would probably be the best person to approach. You could pay him to apply the correct fertilizer to the grass and to chain-harrow the ground to disperse any over-looked droppings and expose the eggs and larvae of worm parasites to the light and cold which will kill them. The farmer might also help you make hay from the part of the ground that is 'resting'.

Worms

Worms can be a very real problem in ponies and horses. So, although this may seem an unpleasant subject, it has to be tackled. Ponies tend to eat the eggs and larvae of parasitic worms as they graze. The adult worms then get into the ponies' guts. The ponies lose condition and may get colic. To offset this a pony should be wormed at least three times during the year – at the beginning and end of the winter, and again during the summer. If your pony is sharing a field with several others worming needs to be carried out even more frequently – at intervals of six to eight weeks is advisable. (See Chapter Eight – Ailments and Accidents.)

Three

A PONY OF YOUR OWN?

To own a pony is wonderful. It is also a responsibility. Before you and your parents take the fateful decision actually to buy a pony all the ways and means should be gone into thoroughly.

First: are you ready for a pony of your own?

Have you had enough practical experience with other people's ponies? Have you learned to ride properly? Have you ever looked after somebody else's pony, or helped in the work of a local riding school?

Pony-trekking or riding holidays can help give you experience. Most establishments allot each guest a pony for the week and it is the rider's task to care for, groom and feed the pony, inspect its feet, tack up and generally look after his or her own mount.

It helps a great deal, of course, if either or both of your parents are horseminded. If not, you can only try to arouse their interest. Get them to come along with you to the riding school. Perhaps persuade them to accompany you on a pony-trek when on holiday. Introduce them to the parents of other pony-owning children.

Subscribing to a pony-orientated magazine can be a great help, too. Read all you can about horses and ponies and try to encourage your parents to do so. Book knowledge on its own is not enough, but it can be useful in conjunction with practical experience. It can also help to arouse a grown-up's interest in the subject.

Once you have got your parents' approval to the idea of your owning a pony then is the time to sit down with them and work out the details.

Counting the cost

Draw up a budget, working out not only the probable cost of buying the pony but adding on all the likely expenditure.

Some ponies are sold with saddle and bridle. If not, a saddle and bridle will have to be bought. You will need buckets, a halter and grooming kit at the very least. Then, unless you are lucky enough to have a field or paddock, there will be the cost of grazing. Possible vet's bills and medicines have to be included. Ponies are hardy animals but sooner or later you are bound to have to call in the vet, if only for advice and help over regular worming.

Shoeing, too, is costly. If you are lucky, and do not do a great deal of road work, you may get a set of shoes to last for five or six weeks. Some ponies need shoeing every month. In between they may lose a shoe. Even if the pony was turned out to grass for a month or two while you were at boarding school its feet would still need attention. Also someone would need to visit the field every day to check that all was well: to fill up the water trough, catch the pony, inspect it for any possible injury or trouble, check the fences, etc. You cannot just go away and forget all about a pony any more than you can any other animal.

Remember also that the pony should be insured, to cover against injury to itself, its rider or any other person.

When you are working out your budget do, please, be honest with yourselves and your parents. It is no use being over-optimistic. Don't forget to budget for hay and additional feed during the winter. In December, January and February even the smallest pony will need twelve pounds of hay or more a day, with two pounds of pony cubes plus bran, if it is to be ridden regularly. Apart from May, June, July and August when the grass is really good, some supplementary diet is usually needed to keep a pony fit and up to work. (See Chapter Four on The Pony's Diet.)

Far too many ponies are kept in unsuitable conditions – perhaps because the children and their parents are not sufficiently knowledgeable or because they cannot really afford the expense involved. They want a pony at all costs and so the pony suffers.

I have known of ponies kept in garages; ponies searching for grass in a miserable quarter-of-an-acre rectangle behind a junk yard; ponies standing fetlock deep in a muddy bog on ill-drained land for much of the year. One poor animal was kept on a tiny strip of land beneath a motorway fly-over where the sun never reached its back and where the only grass was rank and sour.

Some owners, having no idea of a pony's real needs, try to eke out its diet with stale bread, packets of half-mouldy breakfast oats, damaged cans of rice puddings, vegetable scraps and leftovers. I'm sure none of you would try to keep a pony on such unsuitable food but I feel I must point out what can happen when the family budget just isn't able to stretch far enough.

Far better, if you cannot afford to keep a pony properly, to settle for helping at a riding stable or to combine with a pony-owning friend and get your equine enjoyment that way.

Joining the Pony Club

As far as learning about ponies and improving your riding is concerned, the best step anyone can take is to join the Pony Club. There are branches throughout the British Isles, the Isle of Man and in many other countries of the world. All branches have knowledgeable helpers and instructors, lectures, tests, games, outings, and probably camps where you and your parents can meet other keen pony people and have access to plenty of sound and willingly-given advice. If you don't know of a branch near you, why not write to the Pony Club at its headquarters: National Equestrian Centre, Stoneleigh, Kenilworth, Warwickshire CV8 2LR.

Anyone under twenty can join. For a modest yearly subscription you are entitled to wear the Pony Club Badge and tie, and to attend all the meetings, camps and activities organised by your local branch. You will receive much sound practical advice on everything to do with ponies. Some rallies may be purely instructional, others may be fun events. Even if you do not own a pony you can still join. Many riding schools organise rallies for pupils who are Pony Club members. Others provide ponies to hire for the mounted events.

Through the Pony Club you will learn all about stable management, care of the pony's feet, feeding and tack; as well as how to ride properly, progressing to simple dressage and to jumping – even to take part in the mounted games competition heats, the winners of which compete at the Horse of the

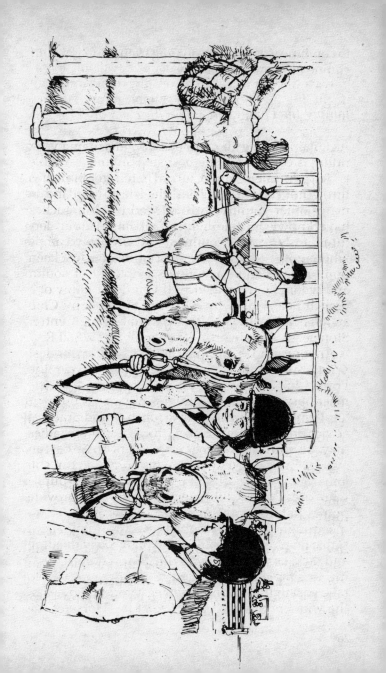

Year Show for the Prince Philip Cup.

Local branch officials are usually available to give advice and practical help on any pony problem, including the choosing of a suitable pony. You may find that a fellow member has a pony for sale because he has become out-grown or because the member is ready for a more advanced or demanding 'ride'.

Some branches of the Pony Club keep a list of ponies in their district which are for sale. Usually the Branch Secretary or the District Commissioner will be able to advise on the suitability of any such pony. Even so, it is always as well to have the animal examined by a vet of your own choosing before completing the purchase.

Buying a Pony From a Riding School

Many riding schools offer ponies for sale from time to time. This can be very satisfactory, particularly if the school is local and with a good reputation to keep up. A considerable advantage is that you should be able to hire the pony and try it out well before you decide. Such a pony will usually be thoroughly reliable and able to act as 'school-master' while you gain experience.

On the debit side, some riding school ponies are only used to going out in a string and may be unhappy and difficult on their own. That is why, before completing any purchase, you should ask to try the pony on its own and take it for a long and varied ride – well past the usual turning-back point for the school ponies. Such a test will soon reveal whether the pony is likely to be a happy purchase or not.

Buying at Auction

This is more chancy. However strong-minded and wary you may be about not allowing your heart to rule your head there is still the chance that on the day you buy some poor, unhappy pony out of pity. True, there have been cases where good food and loving care have turned a sorry purchase into a satisfactory pony. But it is always a gamble. On the other side of the coin, and even more dangerous, you might have your head turned by a splendid-looking pony and buy it without the chance of a sufficient trial only to find when you get it home that it has some vice – is difficult to catch, tricky to groom, apt to rear, an incurable shier, or to be so far beyond your capabilities that instead of feeling comfortable and at home with your new pony you find it a constant source of anxiety and despair.

If you are a really experienced pony person and have somebody even more knowledgeable to guide you, then there is just the chance of your picking up a genuine bargain at auction. Even then you should make sure that the pony has been subject to a veterinary examination, in which case, be sure to inspect the certificate which should have been lodged with the auctioneer.

Buying through advertisement

You could advertise in your local newspaper for the kind of pony you want. Such an advertisement might read:

Wanted. For a good home. Child's first (or second) pony. Must be quiet in traffic and easy to catch and groom. Height 12h2 (or whatever). 'Aged' not objected to but must be under 14 years.

('Aged' by the way means that the pony is 8 years old or more.)

You then sift through the replies with your parents; and go to see and to try out the pony you think is the most promising. Ask permission for a vet of your choice to inspect the animal and take his advice as to purchase.

On the other hand, you may answer an advertisement that appeals to you. You will often see ponies advertised in the local newspaper and in the pony press. It is usually best to pick a pony that can be seen locally. Otherwise you might have a long and disappointing journey only to find when you got there a pony that was quite unsuitable for your purpose or that you didn't even like the look of.

The Purchase

When you go to see a pony that you are thinking of buying do take some experienced and thoroughly pony-wise grown-up with you. Before actually buying any pony it must be given a thorough trial.

Don't be influenced by seeing the pony's present owner or some other child ride the pony. She might be more experienced than you and so the pony might behave better with her or perform better. If your grown-up adviser is light-weight get him or her to try out the pony and then ask to ride it yourself.

Talk to the pony, make friends with it and then put it through its paces. If you are experienced and are buying the pony as a jumper, ask to try it over one or two suitable jumps.

Veterinary Examination

If, after a trial you decide that you like the pony and want to buy, then ask if the owner would be willing to have it passed by a vet. The fee for this examination will be your responsibility but, believe me, the money will be well spent. Choose a veterinary surgeon who is known to be experienced with horses – not all vets have 'horsey' practices – and ask him to examine the pony to see whether a certificate of soundness is warranted.

Such an examination should cover sight, heart, wind, lameness, skin and condition. If no disability is found, the vet will then certify the animal as sound. On the other hand, if some defect should exist the vet will be able to advise you as to whether it is likely to affect the pony's performance in respect of the type of work you will want it to do.

Be quite frank as to the purpose for which you require the pony. Not all forms of unsoundness render a pony unworkable or unsafe, but any defect will detract from the animal's value and should be reflected in the price. For instance, some slight and non-progressive impairment of vision might exist, but the pony might have so accommodated itself to the defect that its performance might in no way be affected. On the other hand a pony blind on one side might be in considerable danger in the face of oncoming or overtaking traffic.

Occasionally a pony might suffer from roaring or whistling in the wind which, though alarming, might in no way affect its performance or staying power. On the other hand, 'broken wind' (an actual tear in the lung) is a serious defect making the pony incapable of sustained effort. Such ponies usually have a persistent hollow cough. It is a safe rule never to buy a coughing pony.

Any lameness, too, must be suspect. Of course all ponies are likely to go lame occasionally through a muscle strain or injury. Such lameness is usually passing. However, a great deal of lameness results from permanent weakness in tendons, ligaments or joints. Many children's ponies are subject to laminitis, a serious disease of the feet. Any pony which has suffered from this disease should be rejected. If the owner states that the lameness is due to a recent strain, leave the pony for a week or two and then ask to try it again and get the owner to give you a warranty that the pony is not chronically or recurrently lame.

Thinness is another reason for turning down a pony. The poor condition could be due to some disease. On the other hand, some ponies are poor 'doers' and, although quite healthy will never look well however much extra feeding and care they receive. Constitutionally thin ponies may be too poor to stay out at grass during the winter. A comfortable rotundity helps to keep the cold at bay.

On the other hand beware of getting a pony that is too fat. Too much weight on a pony's feet is a common cause of laminitis.

Other factors

What do you want of your pony? If you are not very experienced and want a jolly, kindly, easy pony on which to go for rides, attend Pony Club rallies and camps, enter mounted games at gym-khanas and perhaps do a little unambitious jumping, then a twelve year old 'family' pony that has been outgrown by its original owners might well fill the bill. Such a pony should not be too expensive and should not cause you too many anxieties. It should be hardy, healthy, easy to ride and not subject to any form of nerves.

Beware, however, of buying too cheap a pony. 'Bargains' usually have something wrong with them. They may be difficult to box or shoe, apt to go lame, have faulty vision or may even be plain bad-tempered. More about this later. Meanwhile if you are a more experienced and ambitious rider then the typical 'second' pony may do for you. Here you should be looking for a pony with a little more 'go' but at the same time one that is free from dangerous or tiresome vices.

Rearing, bolting, persistent shying, kicking, biting and nipping are all cardinal faults that should put the pony out of court as regards purchase. Shying may be due to defective vision, the result of an accident, fright or simply naughtiness. As a child I occasionally rode a pony called Gypsy who would shy at any dark patch on her near side. This continual 'spooking' was obviously the result of impaired vision. In those days when there was not so much traffic it was merely a nuisance. In present day conditions it could be extremely dangerous.

Other bad faults – sufficient to turn down a possible purchase – would be if the pony were known to be difficult to shoe or box, a persistent bucker or difficult to catch.

A good, trouble-free pony might be described in an advertisement as a 'patent-safety', or a 'school-master' – both terms which could be applicable to a first or second pony. Even if you are a more experienced rider, provided the pony is not sluggish and can jump and do all that you require of it, such descriptions should not prejudice your choice. For a livelier ride look out for the pony described as 'generous', a 'true Christian' or 'genuine in every way', 'quiet to shoe and box', 'easy to catch'.

On the other hand, phrases such as, 'not a novice ride', 'for an experienced rider' or a 'strong ride' should ring warning bells.

'To a good home only', 'owner sadly outgrown' or 'owner looking for Grade A jumper' indicate a genuine reason for the sale and an affection that probably exists between the owner and the pony who will have given several happy years of service. Such a pony will no doubt do just the same for you.

Hardiness

If a pony is to live out all the year round, hardiness is a prime requirement. This means you should be looking for a native mountain or moorland pony or cob. Welsh, Exmoor, Dartmoor or New Forest ponies are all lovely, but here the problem may be one of size. Dartmoor and Exmoor ponies are seldom above 12.2 h.h. New Forest ponies average around 13 h.h., although some which have been hand-reared may reach up to 14.2 h.h. Welsh ponies range up to 13 h.h. Such ponies will suit many under-fourteen year olds.

Some children, however, are tall for their age and this is where problems begin. The choice may then lie among such native breeds as the Dales and Fell ponies and the Highlanders, which are very strongly built, the Connemara ponies, some of which are lighter in build but vary in height from around 13 hands up to a full 15 hands, or perhaps, a Welsh cob. These make marvellous ponies for older children and are often good jumpers.

Alternatively you might consider a part-bred pony which may have had a native mare for its mother but been fathered by a larger horse – often a hunter or maybe a well-known jumper or thoroughbred. Such an animal will need more experienced management than the pure-bred native pony and will be less hardy. Its coat will not be as thick. So, if it is to be kept at grass throughout the year it will probably need to be provided with a New Zealand rug for the cold weather (see Chapter Seven).

Four

BAD WEATHER AND DIET

The natural food of any pony is grass, but in these islands the grass is at its best only for part of the year.

It is the nature of a pony to graze from dawn to dusk but as the nights draw in towards winter the daylight fades earlier, the dawn comes later and so there is less grazing time. For these reasons it is necessary to supplement a pony's diet for a good part of the year.

In early summer, May and June

The grass is growing now and at its most nutritious; the pony will not need any extra food. In fact it will often be necessary to shut the pony away from the field for part of the day. (See Chapter Two) Small ponies that become too fat on too much rich grass often suffer from laminitis.

July to November

In these months the grazing should still be good enough for a pony to manage without extra help except during the school holidays when it has more work to do. With Pony Club rallies, picnic rides, gymkhanas, and perhaps showing, the pony will be away from its grazing for long hours. It will need a concentrated short feed of pony nuts mixed with chaff or bran to keep it going during the day. It will catch up with its bulk roughage (i.e. grass) later because it can graze for most of the summer nights.

November to Mid-December

At this time of year, the pony will need hay once a day. At weekends, if it is away from its field for a long time taking part in riding activities, it should be given an extra short feed.

Mid-December to April

During this period a pony needs hay once or twice daily. It should certainly be fed twice during frosty or snowy weather. If it has work to do it will also need an additional short feed of concentrates.

Ponies vary, but if yours leads an active life and you want it to be fit for plenty of riding during the Easter holidays then you should give it a short feed each day in addition to its hay from the start of the Christmas holidays onwards.

This is the time of year when ponies most need extra help. The weather is at its coldest. The ponies have used up most of their surplus fat. They will soon be casting their coats. The winds are often chill and the grass has not yet begun to grow. Not to feed at this time causes very real deprivation amounting to cruelty. In even the mildest winters ponies need additional food because there is little goodness in the grass.

How much to feed

This varies according to the size of pony. The Pony

Club recommends the quantities given in the following table:

When to feed

It is important to feed at the same time every day, preferably first thing in the morning and at dusk. If you cannot manage to feed twice then it is the evening feed which is essential.

Of course if the pony is kept near to the house you may be able to supplement with juicy tit-bits such as pieces of carrot or apple sliced lengthwise. Little and often is the ideal, but often too difficult to arrange, rule.

To prevent the food being trampled and muddied or spoiled, hay should be given in a net or rack and cubes in a bucket or feed box. Food must be given regularly as ponies simply cannot understand why they should be fed one day and not the next.

Hay and water

Haynets come in three sizes – small, medium and large. The medium size is best for the average pony and will hold 7 or 8 lbs of hay when stuffed completely full. For very small ponies of under 11 hands use the smallest size net. This will hold up to 3 lbs of hay when stuffed full.

Choose a tarred haynet if possible because it will last longer.

The haynet should be firmly tied to a strong fence or gate or suspended high enough from a post or tree so that the pony cannot catch a foot in it. Remember the haynet will sag as it is emptied.

Months	Hay			Pony Cubes		
	Size of Pony			*Size of Pony*		
	11h or less	*12–14h*	*14.2h*	*11h or less*	*12–14h*	*14.2h*
May, June & July	Nil	Nil	Nil	Nil	Nil	Nil
August & September	Nil	Nil	Nil	1 lb (if working hard)	2lbs (if working hard)	4 lbs
October	5 lbs	8 lbs	10 lbs	½ – 1 lb	1 lb	2 lbs
November	8 lbs	10 lbs	15 lbs	1 lb	2 lbs	3 lbs
December, January & February	12–15 lbs	16–18 lbs (according to work)	18–20 lbs (according to work)	2 lbs	3 lbs (according to work)	5 lbs
March	12–15 lbs	16–18 lbs (according to work)	18–20 lbs (according to work)	1 lb	2 lbs (according to work)	4 lbs
April	8 lbs	10–12 lbs (according to work)	14–15 lbs	1 lb	2 lbs (according to work)	4 lbs

If there are several ponies sharing a field there should be a haynet for each, placed well apart so as to prevent the ponies biting and kicking over the food. If one pony is rather shy and apt to get pushed out of the way it will help to put out an extra net a little way off so that if there is any bullying the less-pushy pony will have something to turn to.

When giving a short feed, too, it is important that each pony should be given a separate box or galvanised container. Portable mangers which hook on to a fence or gate are also good.

Wooden hayracks as used by cattle are strong and useful where there are a number of ponies to be fed.

Hay must be of good quality. Poor, mouldy hay can cause colic. Good hay should be sweet-smelling and slightly greenish to look at. Either Seeds Hay or Meadow Hay will do, provided there is no trace of mould or mustiness. Seeds Hay is specially grown hay which is all *good* grass of good quality Meadow Hay. Meadow Hay is ordinary meadow grass cut, which may contain thistles and coarser grasses. A good grass mixture should contain rye, meadow fescue, timothy, cocksfoot, and sweet vernal. For racehorses Seeds Hay is essential but for the average pony, Meadow Hay is quite adequate. It is, however, best when cut from upland areas. River valleys seldom yield good hay. It is apt to be too wet.

Very fresh hay is indigestible. If you have somewhere dry to keep it, hay should be bought well ahead. It is best not to feed hay until it has stood in the stack for at least six months. Hay that has stood for a year to eighteen months is even better.

Water is most important. A pony should have access to fresh, clean water at all times. If you have no trough it should be possible to buy an iron bucket-holder to clip on to the fence or gate where it is impossible for the pony to knock it over. When coming in from a ride you should always give the pony a chance to have a good, long drink before it is given its short feed. Letting the pony eat first and then offering water can cause *colic*.

Ponies' guts are very easily upset. Ponies need plenty of roughage – grass or hay – and they need to be left in peace to digest it. Never feed a pony within two hours of taking it out for a ride. This is why one gives the short feed after work and not before. A pony is liable to get colic if asked to exercise on a full stomach.

If riding from grass when the grazing is good, it is best to shut or tether the pony away from its field for at least an hour before going out. If this is impossible and you have to ride the pony direct from the field then for the first forty minutes take him only at a slow walk.

Concentrates

Pony nuts or cubes are a balanced concentrated food consisting of varying ingredients such as barley, oats, bran, maize, dried grass, molasses, minerals and vitamins. Different makes vary in their constituents, so study the ingredients and decide which you think is best for your pony. Unless you are a very active and experienced rider doing a lot of jumping and cross-country work you do not want your pony to have too many oats.

Bolting

Hungry or greedy ponies tend to bolt their cubes.

This can lead to choking. A friend of mine nearly lost a young pony in this way. A cube became lodged in the pony's throat and was saved only by the prompt action of a farmer friend who applied hot sacks to relax the pony's throat until the arrival of the vet.

To prevent choking and to offset colic it is important that some chaff, bran or a little molasses be mixed with the nuts so as to slow down the pony's consumption and prevent it 'bolting' its food.

It is necessary, too, for a pony's digestion that it should have roughage with or just before the cubes. Otherwise there is always the risk that the cubes might pack down into a mass in the pony's stomach and cause severe – possibly fatal – colic. Never feed cubes on an empty stomach. Always give hay or other roughage to pick at before the short feed, or else mix a quantity of chaff or bran with the nuts.

Keep block

An economical alternative to feeding pony cubes during the cold weather, especially to small native ponies, is to use a Keep block. This is a tasty, vitamin-mineral block similar to a salt lick which is placed in the pony's field or shelter and helps its digestive system to convert hay or grass into more valuable food.

General hints and warnings

Hay, as we know only too well, is expensive these days and there may be the temptation to delay supplementing the grass-kept pony's diet until later into the winter. This is false economy and could only lead to the pony approaching the coldest time of the year in a thin and run-down condition.

Ponies need to be fit and well to withstand winter. This is the time when they can carry a little surplus fat to help keep out the cold. It is vital to feed hay from the middle of October and to add pony cubes at least from November onwards. Ideally, as shown in the table, feeding of extra hay and nuts should begin at the start of October and carry on until April is out.

If your pony's paddock is poor and the grass sparse or if the area is too small – less than 1½ acres per pony – it may be necessary to feed some hay in summer, too. Some owners use cut grass from an orchard or roadside to supplement the feed. This will do no harm provided the grass is cut long and is really fresh – i.e. cut the same day. Wilted grass can cause colic. Lawn clippings are especially dangerous in this respect. They should never be used. They are too fine and tend to impact in the pony's stomach.

In some districts sugar-beet pulp may be available quite cheaply. Usually sold dried, it must be soaked in water overnight to allow it to swell to its fullest extent. If this is not done it will swell inside the pony and cause very bad colic. Sugar beet pulp is a useful energy source for ponies in cold weather and it also helps to provide roughage. It can be used to help out the pony-nut ration. Turnips and swedes are sometimes fed as an economy measure but as these are 91% water they contain little nourishment and very little fibre. The pony so fed goes short of both food and roughage.

Watching the pony's condition

With experience you should be able to tell at a

glance whether a pony is being fed properly or whether it is having too much or too little.

A well-fed pony has a shiny coat and looks reasonably plump and alert even in winter. You should only just be able to feel its ribs.

On the other hand, if the pony is too full of itself, inclined to be naughty and apt to play up – or even if it is tubby and lazy – then it is having more to eat than its size, or the amount of work it does justifies, and you can try cutting down on the concentrates a little.

A thin pony looks 'poor'. You can see its ribs. Its coat is 'staring'. Its eyes look lack-lustre. It has little interest in what is going on and tends to stand 'tucked up' with its head down and haunches rounded – a picture of misery. Either it is ill, in which case you should get a veterinary surgeon to examine it, or it is not getting enough good food. If it shares a field, other animals may be taking its ration, or perhaps its teeth need attention. It may have worms. In any case it is best to get your vet to look at the pony and advise.

Bran Mash

If a pony is off colour or convalescent – even if it is especially tired after a hard day out, wet through, or has, in the school holidays, done a tiring week's work, it will benefit from and certainly enjoy, a bran mash.

Some dry bran or chaff should always be mixed with pony cubes both to make the pony eat more slowly and to increase the fibre in its diet. Made into a mash the bran is very easily assimilated and so easy on a tired pony's digestion. It is, in effect, partially cooked.

To make the mash, put a couple of pounds of bran into a bucket. Stir in a tablespoonful of salt and mix well. Then add enough boiling water to soak the bran thoroughly. Stir it very well. Cover it with a piece of sacking or cloth and let it cool. After a couple of hours you can give it another good stir and test the temperature with your hand. Run your fingers right through the mash and make sure no scalding pockets remain to burn the pony's mouth.

As a special treat, or to disguise the taste of worming powders or other medicine, carrot sliced lengthwise may be added to the mash. You can also use linseed. About 4 ounces of linseed (which looks like small brown seeds) should be put in a pan and well covered with water, then brought slowly to the boil and kept actually boiling for fifteen minutes. This initial boiling is very important. The heat is then turned down and the pan left to simmer gently for six hours, more water being added as necessary. It should then be left to cool and set into a jelly before being mixed with the bran to make a warm and tasty mash.

Gruel can be fed to a pony after a hard day's work, if it has been competing in a hunter trial or other event, or after a long, wet ride in cold weather. A handful-and-a-half of oatmeal is placed in a bucket and boiling water poured over it. The mixture should then be stirred and left to cool. Use plenty of water so that the gruel is thin enough for the horse to drink. It should be about the consistency of oxtail soup.

During frost and snow

At these times it is impossible for a pony to graze.

Twice daily feeding becomes essential and the ponies should, in addition, be given extra hay. Keep this up, too, when the thaw arrives as the snow will leave the grass muddy or shrivelled.

The water supply must have the ice broken at least three times a day so that the pony can drink.

If the ground is frozen for a long time it can be very hard on the hooves, particularly if a pony is unshod. Bruising may occur and feet should be examined carefully for bruised heels or a bruised sole. Such a condition will need the attention of a blacksmith who will usually fit a piece of leather – perhaps covering the whole foot – with a dressing beneath. The ponie's feet should be examined even more frequently than usual as ice or snow may ball up in them. This has to be picked out so that the pony does not slip. For this reason it is unwise to ride in snowy weather.

If you have to lead a pony in snow, put grease in the hoof. This will help to prevent balling up.

FIVE

FEET AND SHOES

'For want of a nail the shoe was lost – for want of a shoe the foot was lost – for want of a foot the horse was lost.' 'No foot no horse' . . . These and similar sayings were impressed on many of us during our youth. If you've never heard them don't worry. The thing is to understand the vital part that feet, legs and correct shoeing play in the well-being of your pony and consequently in your own enjoyment.

Unfortunately, costs are high these days, but a blacksmith's work is very necessary and his fees have to be included in your budget when you work out the cost of keeping a pony.

A pony with neglected, overgrown, split or cracked hooves; worn, twisted or loose shoes; risen clenches and other ills, is uncomfortable and can be an unsafe ride.

If the hoof starts to grow over the shoe or the shoe presses into the foot or heel, a pony will be in pain and can go lame. Ponies with uncared-for feet often stumble. They may damage themselves by 'brushing'. When a pony's hoof strikes the inside of a fetlock or coronet of another leg it often causes a nasty wound.

The Blacksmith

Every pony should be seen by a farrier (blacksmith)

regularly. Six weeks is the longest time that should elapse between visits. If the pony is doing a lot of

fetlock

pastern

hollow of heel

coronet

heel

wall of foot

road work it may need to be shod every four weeks. Even unshod ponies need to be seen every six weeks so that the farrier can trim their hooves.

The hoof is a horny growth similar to our own finger and toe nails but a great deal thicker and stronger. Like our own nails, it makes continual growth.

A visit to the blacksmith does not necessarily mean a new set of shoes every time. Sometimes the farrier may take off the shoes, re-shape them, trim the feet and then put back the old shoes with a new set of nails to fix them.

If you are away at school, or if the pony is not going to be ridden for a month or two, the farrier may recommend removing all four shoes and leaving the pony unshod. Or he may put tips on the fore feet to prevent the toe from cracking and breaking when the ground is hard. Even while you are away you should make arrangements for the farrier to attend to the pony at least every two months.

Shoeing

These days it is not always necessary to take the pony to the actual smithy. Blacksmiths are few and far between and the journey to the forge might necessitate a ride through heavy traffic. Many districts have a travelling farrier who brings with him a portable gas forge. This is excellent, but some smiths practise 'cold' shoeing, which entails fitting ready made shoes to the pony's feet without means of adjustment. This too often results in the pony's hooves being trimmed to fit the shoe rather than the shoe being heated and worked to fit the foot – not a happy state of affairs if there is any alternative.

Feet

A pony wears shoes to save wear and tear on his feet and to protect them. The wall of the hoof is only about three-quarters of an inch thick and yet it has to bear the pony's full weight. It is important, then, that none of the three-quarters of an inch is pared away unnecessarily. When the smith prepares the pony's foot for the shoe he should take only enough horn from the surface that actually stands on the ground to give a level bearing for the shoe. The rasp should never be used high up on the foot and should be employed on the side only to smooth the 'clenches' or nails. The outer wall of the hoof is covered by a thin layer of varnish-like gluey material which is there to prevent the horn drying out. If this were to be removed by rasping it would be very damaging to the hoof.

The outer layers of the wall of the hoof are insensitive, so the pony feels no pain when they are trimmed or have nails driven through.

Inside the hoof, the horn interleaves with folds of sensitive tissue known as 'laminae'. These nourish the horn and attach it firmly to the rest of the foot. A nail driven too deeply, so that it penetrates the 'laminae', will cause pain. If this happens the pony is said to have been 'pricked'. Pus will often accumulate in the area and it will become very painful. Fairly long treatment and considerable rest will be necessary before the pony is fit for work again. A good farrier can be trusted never to inflict such an injury and one should never allow an untrained person, however helpful their intentions, to knock a nail into a pony's hoof (to try to fix a loose shoe, for instance).

If you lift your pony's hoof you will see the

undersurface largely consists of flaky-looking horn. This is called the sole. The outer part where it joins the wall of the hoof helps to carry the pony's weight. It also serves to protect the sensitive inner sole. This should never be pared.

In the middle of the underside of the hoof towards the rear you will notice a V-shaped leathery piece. This is the 'frog' and it is softer and more sensitive than the sole. The sensitivity lets the pony know when its hoof is actually on the ground as the heel usually hits the ground before the toe. It also acts as a built-in non-slip pad and shock absorber. Some smiths like to trim away the ragged edges of the frog with a paring knife but this is not really necessary.

Fitting the shoe

At one time shoes were individually made by hand and beaten out on the anvil to shape them to fit any particular hoof. Today, most farriers buy ready-made shoes with nail-holes stamped in them. However, no two ponies' feet are exactly alike and it is usually necessary to shape the shoe to fit the feet.

The blacksmith fits the shoe to the foot and then 'burns' it on. Alarming though this sounds and despite the clouds of smoke that arise, few ponies really mind. If they are frightened at first by 'hot' shoeing they will usually get used to it with patience and understanding on your part. If your pony does object, however, it would be a good idea to have a 'horsey' grown-up on hand to help. They cannot feel any heat or discomfort unless the hoof has been badly pared. While the shoe is held to the foot the smith can see whether it fits properly or whether it needs any alterations.

The shoe is cooled and the ends of the metal (the 'heels') filed. Next, the shoe is nailed on with special nails. Most ponies will need five, six or seven nails according to the size of their feet. Horses need more. The nails are driven in very carefully so that they do not pierce the 'laminae'. The pointed ends are then twisted off and the heads ('clenches') neatened.

When the job is finished, no daylight should show between the metal shoe and the horn of the hoof, especially in the heel region.

Picking out the hoof

Between visits to the farrier the pony's feet should be checked each day. Routine grooming should always include 'picking' out the feet with a hoof-pick – a blunt metal hook – to remove any dirt or stones. Scrape the dirt from the foot, beginning at the heel and working towards the toe, carefully cleaning the grooves on either side of the frog. At the same time, notice whether any of the shoes are loose. A 'cast' shoe means that the pony will be walking unevenly on the remaining three. Worse still, a shoe may be so loose that it is hanging on by a single nail and may twist round and make a bad cut on the opposite leg.

Loose shoes can usually be detected by the characteristic 'clicking' sound the pony makes as it goes along a road or other macadamised surface.

Leg injuries

These are sometimes caused by the pony's faulty

action, due to bad shoeing, old age or weak or feeble riding, i.e. not keeping your pony up to the bit but letting him just slop about, or riding at too fast a trot so that he becomes unbalanced. They may also occur in the field, particularly an over-reach (see below) if the hooves are left too long.

One of the commonest wounds is found on the inside of the fetlock and is caused by 'brushing' – that is, one hoof hits the inside of the fetlock or the coronet of another leg and cuts it. If this occurs on more than one occasion the leg that tends to be cut should be protected by a 'brushing boot' – a padded gaiter strapped around the fetlock.

If it is the coronet that receives the injury, an over-reach boot or a Yorkshire boot, worn like a spat, lower down, will give more protection. The

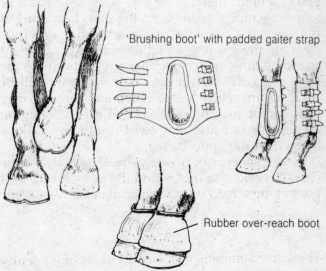

How a 'brushing wound' may occur

'Brushing boot' with padded gaiter strap

Rubber over-reach boot

smith can also help by shoeing the foot that causes the trouble with a 'feather-edged' shoe. This has no nails on the inside edge and the inner edge is very thin in width – much thinner than the outer edge.

Over-reach

This is a similar type of injury, usually occuring at the gallop when the toe of a hind shoe catches the foreleg at the heel or above. Both this and a 'brushing' wound should be treated with an anti-septic dressing. If the skin is broken it is a wise precaution to call the vet and have an anti-tetanus injection administered should the pony not already have been immunised. Rubber over-reach boots that fit round the pastern to protect it should be worn if the pony seems particularly liable to this type of injury.

Six

GROOMING

The grooming of a pony at grass differs from that of a stabled pony in that a pony kept in confinement needs particularly vigorous grooming to tone up its muscles and circulation (all the grease has to be got out of its coat to keep it clean and healthy) whereas a pony living out of doors needs the grease left in its coat to help it keep warm and to protect it from rain and weather.

The main purpose in grooming a pony at grass is to keep it clean and tidy. All healthy ponies have some shine to their coats. In the spring and autumn they shed their coats and then they may look a little rough as the old hair comes away. Superficial brushing with a dandy brush will remove most of this without getting out the natural oil and grease from the coat.

Outdoor ponies should never be brushed too much and this is particularly true when they are changing their coats. Nature's way is for the pony to shed a little hair and then grow a little. The process is gradual and should not be hurried.

Whether the pony is being groomed near the house, in its field, in a shed or stable, it should be tied up, using a quick-release knot, to a piece of breakable string. Then if it takes fright and pulls back it will neither hurt itself nor break the head-collar.

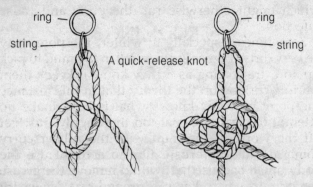

ring

string

A quick-release knot

ring

string

Grooming kit

The basic essential tools for grooming are: a halter (to tie up the pony); bucket (quarter full of cold water); sponge; water brush; dandy brush; body brush and curry comb; sweat scraper; rubber curry comb; hoof pick; a sack (cut and opened out); a surcingle; a bundle of straw; hoof oil and brush; stable rubber and stable bandages for legs and tail.

The first act in grooming a pony should be to pick out its feet to remove any stones and dirt. This is most essential and must never be forgotten. It should also be done before and after a ride.

Routine

The dirt should be scraped from the foot, starting at the heel and working to the toe, being careful to clean out thoroughly the grooves on each side of the frog.

Next use the dandy brush to get the mud off the

body and legs. Wherever the tack – saddle, girth and bridle – touches, must be quite free from dirt, which might otherwise rub the pony and cause infection.

Sometimes, especially in winter, the pony may be very dirty. Ponies seem to roll in the mud to pick up an extra coating as if they know it keeps them warm! Working on the theory that in this instance the pony probably knows what is best, make no attempt to clean the coat too thoroughly. Just get off the worst of the mud with the rubber curry comb and dandy brush. On no account use the body brush because that would remove the grease the pony needs to keep warm and dry. Never try to brush wet mud off a pony's legs and feet. This would only work it into the skin and heels and might cause mud fever. Wait until the mud is dry. Then examine the pony carefully and if necessary sponge the eyes, nose and under the tail. Here again, if sponging is overdone it removes the natural lubrication that keeps these parts moist.

Use the body brush to do the mane and tail, brushing both out thoroughly. Holding the curry comb in the opposite hand, rub it over the body brush as you work to clean out the dirt and scurf. The dirt that accumulates in the curry comb should be tapped out periodically against a wall or on a hard floor. If you are grooming out of doors, take care that the scurf and dirt do not blow back on to the clean pony.

The pony's face is best gently brushed with the body brush. To do this you will need to remove the halter. Place it round the pony's neck. Holding the head-rope in one hand, brush the face and forelock carefully. Then sponge the eyes and nostrils. In summer you might gently smear fly repellent jelly round the eyes to keep off insects. Afterwards restore the halter to its normal position.

Finally, oil the feet, taking care to cover all the horn and across the bulbs of the heels (see diagram of foot).

Grooming of a stabled pony, or thorough grooming before a special event. Stand facing the pony's tail, hold the body brush in the hand nearest the pony and take the curry comb in the other hand. As you brush (using circular movements that follow the lie of the pony's coat) you should make pauses in order to draw the curry comb over the brush and remove the dirt.

A stabled pony

The rigorous use of the body brush is vital, not only to clean the coat but also to act as a massage, toning up the pony's muscles and keeping his circulation going. It should be used with considerable effort, rubbing the brush over the curry comb every six or seven strokes to keep it clean.

At the end of grooming, rub the pony with the stable rubber, which is a clean linen cloth about the size of a tea towel but of coarser, heavier material. This will put a gloss on its coat.

A wet pony

In bad weather or when the pony is sweating after a day's hard work – it is necessary to get the worst of the wet off the neck and body with a sweat scraper. Then rub the pony down with a good handful of straw, working vigorously and using your left hand to dry the near-side (left) of the pony and your right hand for the off (right) as when brushing.

Never rub against the lie of the coat as that always rubs the wet in. *Always* brush or rub the way the coat lies.

To put a saddle on to a wet back leads to all kinds of troubles. Make sure the pony's back and loins are really dry. If the pony is soaking wet it helps to 'thatch' the pony's back. Put some dry, fresh straw or hay all over the pony's back and loins. Then put a piece of sacking or sweat rug (string vest) to keep the straw in place and use a surcingle to hold it in place. Never leave a pony thatched for longer than an hour because back and loins might overheat and become itchy.

While you are waiting for the pony's back to dry use a stable rubber or straw to dry his ears. Pulling them gently will help to bring back the circulation and to warm the pony up. Pick out the feet. Then rub down the legs and pasterns with a handful of straw or hay. If the legs are very wet and muddy put on a set of stable bandages with straw underneath. Then the legs will quickly dry and you can brush off the dry mud with the dandy brush. Finally, with the body brush, brush the mane and tail even if they are still wet. Give the pony water and a haynet to pull at and leave it to dry off for the remainder of the hour.

After you have removed the straw and sacking, the pony should be dry enough to have the rest of the mud brushed off with a dandy brush.

Washing a pony is inadvisable, except for the tail. Occasionally a grey pony or a pony with white legs needs to have stains removed before a show or other special occasion. In this case wet the smallest possible area and wash it with a block of mild soap. *Never* use detergent, which can seriously damage a pony's coat, remove all natural grease and cause irritation. Cracked heels are due to the lazy habit of washing the mud off a pony's legs instead of letting it dry and then brushing it off.

The tail should be washed by dipping it into a bucket of warm water. Soap it in the usual way and then dip it into the water again to rinse it.

After a ride

When you come in from a ride, remove the saddle, give the pony a chance to 'stale' (relieve itself) then brush off the saddle mark and examine the legs and flanks for any hurt. Even the slightest scratch should be treated with wound powder to prevent infection which can rapidly become serious. Always inspect the feet, picking out any grit or stones that might have become embedded in the groove around the frog and check the shoes to make sure they have not become loose. (As stated in Chapter Five a loose shoe can be dangerous, inflicting nasty cuts on the other legs or twisting and tearing the hoof.)

In winter, offer some tepid water but don't worry or wait about if the pony won't touch it. Give it a quick look over for any injury and then turn it out into the field right away. Even if it is raining or pelting with sleet your pony will be glad to have a roll, shake itself, snatch a mouthful of grass and then go to the trough to drink. This helps the pony relax, warm up and dry off, if sweating.

Meanwhile put a feed in its usual place – either in a bucket in the shelter, near the gate or in a clip-on tray attached to the gate or fence. The hay ration should be put in a net, suspended from a ring in the shelter, tied securely to the fence or suspended from a tree at the right height.

Next day catch up the pony and inspect it very carefully for any cuts, thorns, back and girth galls, sore mouth or an injury. Brush off surplus mud and any remaining sweat marks.

Pick out and inspect the feet. Look out for risen clenches or loose or twisted shoes. Then trot the pony up and down a level bit of hard ground or road to check whether there is any lameness.

Check that it ate up its feed. Then turn it out again, giving hay and a short feed as usual.

After a hard day, offer a bran mash and next day give the pony a full day's rest. Let it stay quietly in its field unless in summer the flies are bad. Then the pony will appreciate being in a shelter for part of the day.

Sometimes, before an early start it helps to catch the pony the previous evening and keep it in a stable for the night. The pony must be thoroughly dried beforehand, thatching it if necessary. Then pick out the feet and brush the mane and tail. Proceed as for grooming a wet pony.

Stable care

If it is intended at any time to leave a pony indoors – in a box or stable for the night – you must first put down a good bed of straw, or cut dry bracken or wood shavings; a bucket of water; a short feed (pony nuts and chaff or bran), and some hay.

Leave the top half of the stable door open so that the pony has plenty of air. If there is a window on the same side of the door, that may also be left open. If the window is on the opposite side to the door it had better remain shut. Cross draughts can cause trouble. Native ponies are perfectly fit and hardy out of doors in all weathers but once you bring them in there is the risk, unless they have plenty of air, that they may get a chill.

Once the pony is dry you can cover its back and loins with a thin lightweight rug and a roller to fasten it. Even though the pony has a thick coat and is perfectly all right out of doors where it can move about and seek natural shelter, once it is stabled it may feel cold.

Manes and Tails

A pony's mane and tail are there for its protection. All the same, they need some care to keep them neat. A good, thick, well-trimmed mane will not hold water and lie sodden on the pony's neck. It dries quickly and is easily brushed out. The forelock should seldom be trimmed. Its function is to keep the flies away from the pony's eyes.

Ponies that live outdoors do not usually need their tails 'pulled' or thinned. The tail should be good and full all the way down, but you can neaten the ends by 'banging' (trimming them off square) so that the tail does not trail in the mud. Care must be taken not to cut the tail hairs too short. The tail should come to about a couple of inches below the pony's hocks.

The mane and the tail should both be trimmed in November. They will then keep in good shape throughout the winter. In spring and summer when the hair is growing they may need two or three further trims, but this varies from pony to pony and depends on how fast the hair grows.

Hairy heels

In winter the pony needs the hair round its fetlocks and down the back of the pasterns and heels for protection. In summer it will look smarter if these are trimmed. This job should be done with scissors and comb, taking care to keep the hair lying naturally.

Some ponies have quite long eyelashes. Others have stronger and more numerous whiskers on the muzzle than others. These should never be shortened or cut off. Like a cat, the pony uses its whiskers and eyelashes as feelers in the dark.

The hair inside its ears should be left, too. Its function is to protect the ears against flies and bad weather.

Clipping

Even though a pony lives at grass, if it is to be called upon to do a lot of fast work in the winter it should be clipped trace-high. Provided the clip is done in mid-November so that the coat starts to grow again and the pony becomes used to its clip before the very cold weather, no harm will be done. Care must be taken, though, not to cut away too much coat. The hair should be left low down on the pony's sides. A trace clip means exactly what it says. The clip should stop where the traces would come were the pony harnessed to pull a trap. The full coat should be left on the quarters and around the root of the tail. The legs, of course, will not be clipped, nor should the hair over the gullet and windpipe be removed.

Without such a clip, the pony that is entered for hunter trials, cross-country or endurance rides during the winter will sweat heavily, become very thirsty and probably lose condition.

Plaiting

For a show or other special occasion you may want to plait the pony's mane. To do this you will need a comb, water brush, a pair of blunt-ended scissors, a thick needle and a reel of thread the colour of the mane.

First brush out the pony's mane so that it is quite clean. Then dampen it down with the water brush to make it more manageable. Divide the mane into seven parts with the comb. Plait the first lock tightly

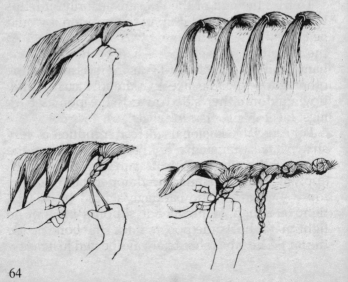

into a pigtail, including the thread in the lower part of the plait. Tie the thread round the end of the plait to keep it from coming undone. Then wind the plait up so that it forms a neat tight knob at the root of the mane. Secure it with needle and thread, sewing it through several times before tying the cotton to fasten off.

Repeat the procedure with each of the remaining sections of the mane.

Tail

To get the tail into a good shape for showing, it may need to be thinned a little at the top. This is done by 'pulling', first brushing the tail and then plucking out by hand a few hairs from the sides and upper part of the dock. Never try to trim the top of the tail with scissors as this can only produce a disastrous effect.

To trim the end of the tail satisfactorily, it helps to get a friend to hold it up in the position it would be carried in when the pony was trotting along. At the same time gather up the hair of the tail in one hand and cut it straight with the scissors in the other. Some people like to slant the cut slightly upwards on either side towards the pony's back legs.

For special occasions you can produce a very shapely tail by using a tail bandage. Roll up the stockinette bandage with its tapes inwards. Then apply it to the brushed and damped tail from the top downwards. The bandage should be wound tightly enough to prevent it slipping but not so tight that it hurts the pony's dock (the bone inside the tail). The tapes should always be tied just below

the end of the dock. The bandage should be left in position for a couple of hours in order to 'set' the tail. Then, to remove it, simply grasp it at the top and slide it off the tail.

Seven

TACK AND ITS CARE

To buy new tack these days is expensive. Saddles, in particular cost a great deal so there is much to be said for buying second-hand. You will often see advertisements in the local paper or the pony press. A good, well-kept saddle, even though it may be a little worn, is a sound investment and will often prove more comfortable than a new one with hard, slippery leather that has to be worked and worn in before you feel secure. However, when buying a second-hand saddle always get an expert to check it. The saddle tree can get twisted – i.e. become slightly sloping one way or the other – which will give the pony a sore back.

The saddle must be a good fit, also, or it may slide about and give the pony sores. A saddle is meant to keep the rider's weight off the pony's spine. This is why it is built on a frame or 'tree'. This used to be made of wood but nowadays it is constructed of metal, with a central arch over the pony's backbone. The rider's weight is carried on a padded lining which sits on the thick muscles at either side of the pony's spine.

A saddle that is too narrow cannot sit properly. It will probably stick up in front and pinch the pony's withers.

On the other hand, if the saddle is too wide it will slip about and, apart from being insecure for the rider, will give the pony a sore back. If the saddle is much too big there is nothing that can be done about it. But a saddle that is only slightly too large can often be made to fit comfortably by the use of a 'numnah', a saddle-shaped pad of felt or sheepskin. Pads of quilted nylon are also obtainable but sheepskin or felt is best. The important thing is for the numnah to be pulled up well clear of the pony's spine and into the arch of the saddle. The saddle's fit may also be helped by a piece of sheepskin over the pony's withers. Care must be taken to check that the sheepskin is flat and not wrinkled otherwise it might cause galling.

Try if you can to get a leather lined saddle. Serge or other cloths are less hard-wearing and may need trips to the saddler for repair.

The girth

This is used to hold the saddle in place. Your safety depends on its soundness. Unless you buy a saddle with a sound and serviceable leather girth you should buy a new one of good quality, *soft* nylon string. This is flexible, comfortable for the pony, unlikely to cause galling and is easy to wash. Such girths last a long time. Cheap nylon girths can become very narrow, twist and cut into the pony. Cottage craft girths are usually good. Webbing girths should be avoided as they tend to break suddenly, usually at a crucial time, and can cause accidents.

The stirrups

These consist of 'irons' into which you put your feet and 'leathers' – straps holding them and attaching them to the saddle.

It is most important that the irons should be big enough for you easily to kick your feet free in times of trouble. Some stirrup irons are of a 'safety type' with a rubber band on one side which comes away should pressure be put on it if the rider is in danger of being dragged along with one foot in the stirrup.

The leathers pass through the slot on top of the iron and are secured to the saddle by a bar which usually has a snap-up fastening. This catch should always be left down so that if the rider is dragged the leather can slide free of the bar.

The crupper

Some ponies have narrow withers and shoulders so that their saddles tend to slip forward. To prevent this they wear a crupper – a strap which buckles to a D ring at the back of the saddle and is looped at the other end to pass round the base of the pony's tail. The crupper is put on after the saddle. When fastened room should be left for a hand to be passed between the strap and the pony's rump. Understandably any pony would object to a crupper that fitted too tightly and might well show its discomfort by bucking.

Saddling up

It is usual to fasten the pony to a breakable piece of string by its halter with a quick release knot before you put on the saddle.

Before saddling always run the stirrups up the leathers so that they cannot bang about and startle the pony. Draw the girth up over the seat and carry the saddle on your bent arm. Always put the greasy side of the girth over the saddle. Mud scratches but grease will wash off.

As you go up to the pony, take the saddle in both hands. Place it well forward on the pony's withers and slide it back into place so that the hair lies smooth underneath. Saddling is always done from the near side, that is from the left, facing the pony's head.

To make sure the pony is comfortable, take each foreleg in turn and stretch it forward to pull any wrinkles of skin from under the girth. Then tighten the girth, checking the tightness at the lowest point beneath the pony's chest. Some ponies have a trick of blowing themselves out so that the girth is too slack. To prevent this, smooth down the hair beneath the girth by running a finger between the girth and the pony, walk the pony forward a couple of steps so that it relaxes and then check the tightness again, pulling up the girth a hole or two if necessary.

If you are using a folded leather girth make sure the free edge is at the back. Used the other way round it will cut and chafe the pony's skin.

If you are using a numnah, put it into position before you add the saddle. Place the numnah forward on the withers and then slide it back. Pull the numnah up into the saddle arch and buckle the pony's girth before fastening the tapes attaching the numnah to the saddle.

When unsaddling always run the irons up the leathers first. Then unfasten the girth and fold it across the seat of the saddle before you take it off.

The bridle

Most ponies go well in an ordinary *snaffle*. This is

the simplest form of jointed bit attached to two loose metal rings that join it to the bridle on either side. The bit acts on the bars of the mouth and the lips to give control of the pony by a squeezing action across the lower jaw.

A more sophisticated form of snaffle, the *jointed eggbutt*, has specially designed rings to prevent pinching of the pony's lips. Seldom seen these

days, but very cruel, is the *twisted snaffle* in which the bit has serrated edges that cut into the pony's mouth. Needless to say, this bit should never be used.

Bridling

When putting on the bridle always leave the throat-lash and nose-band unbuckled. First put the reins over your pony's head. Then remove his halter. Hold the head-piece in your right hand and the bit in your left. Bring up your right hand holding the headpiece to the level of the pony's ears. Then, with your left hand, press the bit against the pony's teeth to cause him to open his mouth. Press in the bit and at the same time bring the head-piece over and behind his ears. Next fasten the throat-lash and then the nose-band, making sure that the nose-band is beneath the cheek piece of the bridle.

The bit should be high enough in the pony's mouth so as to touch but not wrinkle the corners.

To take the bridle off, unfasten the throat-lash and nose-band, take the reins in your right hand, bring that same hand up to the head-piece, draw the head-piece over your pony's ears and let the bit drop out of his mouth.

The dropped noseband

Some ponies are inclined to pull, so to enable the rider to keep better control some people use a 'dropped' noseband with their jointed snaffle. Many ponies do very well in this combination. It is important to see that the front part of the noseband is high enough not to interfere with the pony's breathing. It should fit above the soft part of the pony's nose.

The strap of the dropped noseband buckles below the bit but it should not be buckled too tightly. There should be a little room between the strap and the crease of the jaw. The idea is not to bind the pony's mouth tight shut but just to prevent him opening it too far and so evading the bit.

Martingales

These are used to regulate a pony's head carriage. The 'running' martingale is a strap with a loop at one end to which the girth is attached. It passes between the pony's front legs and up its chest where it divides into two, with rings at the end through which the reins are passed. An additional strap goes round the pony's neck to support the martingale. A running martingale prevents a pony tossing his head up above the level of control by evading the action of the bit.

It is most important to ensure that the rings of the martingale cannot run up the reins and get hooked round the rings of the bit. This is done by threading rubber stops on to the reins. When

nose band

martingale

correctly fitted the straps with the rings should be long enough to reach the withers when the martingale is in position, attached to the girth.

A 'standing' martingale is similar to a running martingale but, in place of the two straps with rings through which the reins pass, there is a single strap which is fitted free of the reins and attached to the noseband. This martingale must never be used with a drop noseband. It should be used with a 'cavesson' noseband which is buckled above the bit and under the cheek pieces of the bridle. The noseband should always be fastened loosely enough to admit the width of two fingers between it and the pony's jaw.

A standing martingale's function is to prevent the pony tossing its head in the air and banging its rider in the face. Like the running martingale it also prevents the pony carrying its head too high for easy control.

Apart from the martingales you can use a simple neck strap, possibly a spare stirrup leather, buckled round the pony's neck to give you a hold when jumping if you feel insecure. This is particularly helpful because you can hold on to it along with the reins and so prevent yourself giving the pony a jab in the mouth if you are thrown off balance.

The 'Irish' martingale is a strap about six inches long with a ring at each end through which the reins are passed beneath the pony's neck. This simply prevents the reins being thrown over the pony's head.

Care of Tack

Saddlery needs to be well looked after. Neglected

tack cracks, becomes uncomfortable for the pony, chafes, and, in time, becomes unsafe. Tack should be cleaned every time after use so as to remove all salty sweat and the layers of mud and dirt which would otherwise accumulate.

Tack should always be taken to pieces for cleaning. The bit and stirrup irons should be scrubbed with warm water, dried and polished. The saddle should be turned over and its lining brushed free of hairs and grease. Both saddle and bridle should then be washed with lukewarm water and saddle soap. Never use detergent, as this would harden and spoil the leather. Let the saddle and bridle dry, then rub in a harness dressing or saddle soap to keep the leather supple. This will preserve the stitching and prevent the leather going stiff and board-like if it gets soaked with rain.

Be careful not to use too much soap or grease as this might build up into a hard layer which would chafe the pony's skin.

You may be offered second-hand tack which might have been kept indoors in too warm an atmosphere and gone hard and dry. It can be worked supple again with a hide dressing or leather oil. Once this has soaked in, saddle soap the leather. Undo all the buckles and put the reins and bridle in an old stocking soaked in neatsfoot oil.

If you are not going to ride for some time coat the leather with Vaseline before putting it away. This will prevent it from drying out.

Nylon string girths can be washed and hung up to dry overnight. Webbing girths and numnahs, like serge saddle-linings, should be brushed with the dandy brush. Saddle cloths, blankets and wither pads should receive frequent washing.

Storing Tack

Leather needs to be kept in a fairly dry atmosphere. In the old days, tack rooms had a constantly burning stove which kept the saddles aired during bad weather. Today the best you can probably do is to keep it in a warm and airy (not overheated) part of your house. A slightly heated garage or utility room is ideal. If leather gets too hot it becomes brittle. On the other hand if it is left in a cold, damp place, it absorbs water and feels clammy. In a warm, damp atmosphere it may even start to go mouldy.

Saddles should always be kept on saddle racks to preserve their shape. Lightweight, free-standing racks can be bought or you can buy cheaper metal racks which can be fixed to the wall. If you are clever with your hands you can make a wooden saddle rack or persuade your parents or a handyman friend to construct one for you. The important thing is that it should provide a firm, roof-shaped ridge on which the saddle can sit.

Bridles should always be hung up by the headpiece. You can buy a proper bridle hook for this purpose or you can knock in two nails about five centimetres apart. Even better is an empty tin 4" in diameter nailed to the wall. Make sure the hook is high enough to prevent the reins trailing on the ground. Stirrup leathers should be hung from nails by their buckles. Irons too, will easily loop over a nail or hook.

New Zealand rugs

These are designed as weatherproof coats enabling ponies that would not otherwise be able to live out during the winter to do so.

Native ponies, though, are better off without such covering. Their own coats are thick, the hair fluffing out naturally in cold weather with a duvet effect – a layer of air being trapped in the hair to keep the pony warm. Mountain and moorland crosses such as the Welsh-Arabian, or ponies with thoroughbred blood, have finer coats. They really do need New Zealand rugs if they are to winter outside.

The snag is that not all so-called 'New Zealand' rugs measure up to the true specification. Poor ones let through the wet. They may chafe the withers. Sometimes the straps are insecurely sewn with the result that the pony gets tangled up in them, panics and may hurt himself.

The answer is to buy the very best you can afford. Greenham is a good name to watch for.

A true New Zealand rug should be made of waterproof canvas with a wool lining. It should have two strap fastenings at the chest, preferably made of waterproof chrome leather which does not need oiling. Leg straps which pass between the pony's hind legs are attached at each side. These help to hold the rug in place. Some New Zealand rugs have a surcingle attached but this can cause pressure on the withers. It may be best to unpick them at the withers and slip in a sponge or wither pad to prevent rubbing. Alternatively, you could sew sheepskin pieces inside the rug along the withers and shoulders where rubbing might occur. The sheepskin will get wet, of course, and so will the rug. However waterproof it is stated to be, no pony should be left in a sodden New Zealand rug. You need two so that one can be drying while the other is in use.

Ponies wearing New Zealand rugs should be checked at least twice a day in case it is necessary to straighten the rugs.

The two rugs should be changed every day – giving the one you have taken off a chance to dry out and air. Look the rugs over for tears or damaged stitching and have these mended quickly. Sometimes you can replace the stitching yourself, using the existing holes and a waxed thread. If you do your own repairs always rub over the stitches with candlewax to make them waterproof.

Once the rug is completely dry, brush the inside thoroughly to remove hairs and mud and then brush off any mud from the outside.

Sweat rug

This is the pony's string vest! Every pony should have one. The rug is made of an open cotton mesh and can be used when you bring your pony home too hot – as we all do at times. Fasten the rug into place with a surcingle and leave it on while the pony has a drink of warm water and, if he has had a heavy day, a ready prepared bran mash. If the pony is very wet, put a thatching of straw beneath the sweat rug to help him to dry more quickly. Do not leave the rug in place too long. After an hour the pony will usually be dry enough for you to brush off the worst of the mud and to turn him into his field.

Eight

AILMENTS AND ACCIDENTS

Ponies, like the rest of us, are subject to occasional illness, sprains, bruises, coughs, colds and colic. Some of these complaints are minor. Many you can learn to treat for yourself. Some, however, must always be taken seriously. Chief among these are coughs, respiratory infections and colic. Unlike the occasional tummy-ache which you or I might get, colic in ponies must always be regarded as a danger signal. Neglected, it can lead to a twisted gut and that could mean either a surgical operation or the pony having to be put down.

Colic

Ponies are very sensitive to digestive upsets, usually caused by incorrect feeding – giving cubes without additional roughage such as chaff or bran mixed in for instance – or by letting them gorge too much fresh, spring grass.

A pony with colic becomes restless and fidgety. He looks, and is, worried. He peers round at his flanks, stamps and kicks at his belly. Additionally he may paw the ground, pant, sweat and swish his tail.

The answer is to call the vet at once. It is a waste of time to try to dose the pony yourself. While you are waiting for the vet to arrive, walk the pony about. Keep it on the move. On no account must it be allowed to lie down and roll, which is what it will try to do, and which could result in the dreaded twisted gut.

If the weather is cold, put on a rug. Do not leave the pony alone for a minute but get someone else to prepare an emergency stable, putting down deep straw, wood shavings, or cut bracken. If it is dark, ask your helper to make sure that there is a light by which the vet can work.

Try to discover exactly what has caused the colic so that you can prevent it happening again.

Other signs which should lead you to call the vet

You can usually tell if a pony is sick because he will look miserable. He will stand with his head and tail down, his quarters under him, looking 'tucked up'. His coat will be dull and staring. His ears will be half-way between forward and back. He will take little interest in what is going on around him. He may be off his food, taking only water. He could be shivery and cold, or hot with sweat breaking out in patches. There may be a watery, or worse still a thick, discharge from the eyes or nose. The pony may be breathing hard and panting. Any of these symptoms mean he is in need of help and you should call the vet immediately. Running eyes and nose may be caused by a cold. Or the pony may have flu, which could lead to pneumonia. He could even have 'strangles'.

Strangles is an acutely contagious (catching) disease of the nose and throat with swelling of the glands. This swelling may even occur in other parts of the body. There will be a thick, white discharge from the nostrils and the eyes will be inflamed.

Strangles is a streptococcal infection which most frequently attacks young animals under 6 years old. The infection can be carried in food. It may also be found in stables or mangers, travelling boxes or paddocks which have been used by an infected horse or pony. Head collars, bedding, buckets, and grooming kit may also carry the trouble, so everything must be disinfected and the pony kept in isolation until it recovers. It is essential to get veterinary advice as soon as possible because neglected cases can lead to the death of the pony.

It is better always to be sure than sorry. If you are a new pony owner you may sometimes call the vet unnecessarily. Don't worry. You will soon learn from experience when the pony is really ill and when he has just some minor ailment you can treat yourself. Far better to have the odd unnecessary vet's bill than to lose your pony. All ponies need to be seen by the vet from time to time if only to ensure that their teeth are checked and any rough edges filed so that they can make the best use of their food. Also they must be given their regular immunization jabs, against flu, tetanus etc.

Most vets are good at explaining, particularly when a pony has an interested owner. You will learn something from each visit until you become experienced enough to tell at a glance whether anything is wrong with the pony for yourself and to be able to decide exactly what action to take.

Cuts and Wounds

These small injuries may vary from surface scratches to deep slashes or puncture wounds that need veterinary attention. Simple cuts and grazes should be washed clean with cold water to which a teaspoon of common salt has been added. If the cuts are neglected flies may infect them in summer – or mud in winter – and cause festering. Heavy bleeding needs the vet and should meanwhile be staunched by finger pressure on a thick pad of gauze or cotton wool. To protect surface cuts and grazes smear on zinc ointment, acriflavine cream or dust with antiseptic powder.

To stop bad bleeding

Bad bleeding can be frightening, and it needs prompt treatment if the pony is not to be weakened. Most bleeding can be stopped by pressure on the wound. First place a pad of lint, or a folded clean handkerchief on the wound and bandage it tightly. A penny or flat stone may be used on top of the pad to give additional pressure. Otherwise apply finger pressure. If you are out for a ride and have no bandage, use a scarf or tie. Bandaging tightly above and below the wound may help to stop the bleeding.

Sometimes a pony may receive such a deep cut that an artery is severed. Bright red blood pumps out fast and the pony could bleed to death if immediate action is not taken. Such a gash is usually on a leg and the remedy is to apply a tourniquet. This is done by folding and tying a large handkerchief above the wound (between the gash and the heart) and twisting a stick or riding switch in it until it is tight enough to stop the circulation – and the bleeding. This cannot be kept up for too long. The vet must be called but until he comes it is necessary to keep the tourniquet in position, releasing the

pressure every quarter of an hour to prevent the limb becoming gangrenous and then tightening it again before too much blood can be lost. The tourniquet should be released for between one and two minutes – no longer – and should be replaced a little higher up or lower down the limb from where it was originally placed so as to minimise further damage to the tissues.

Severe bleeding always needs a vet.

For first aid purposes you should always carry two large clean handkerchiefs (men's size), a spare bandage, a tie, scarf, or even a length of cord.

Warbles

These lumps sometimes occur on the pony's back

in January. They are caused by the warble fly which lays its eggs on an animal's back in the summer, leaving them to hatch later into grubs. The lumps should be fomented with kaolin (not too hot) to draw out the maggots and pus. The pony must not be worked.

Other Lumps

These may be a sign that a thorn is present or they may be the result of a kick or blow. If the pony has picked up a thorn, bathe the place frequently with warm water and smear a warm (*not too hot*) kaolin poultice on a piece of greaseproof paper, taping it in place with strips of elastoplast. Alternatively an elastoplast wound dressing can be applied, well smeared with warm kaolin. To heat the kaolin, place it in a saucepan of water. Bring it to the boil, and allow it to simmer for ten minutes, stirring it so as to distribute the heat evenly through the poultice. The kaolin should be warm but not hot enough to cause pain and should be tested cautiously on the back of the hand before being smeared thickly on to a piece of greaseproof paper and taped into place on the pony.

If the lump has been caused by a kick or blow there is bound to be some bruising present. Your fingers will be able to detect heat in the place which will be sore to touch, making the pony flinch. In this case the treatment is to trickle cold water very slowly from the garden hose from well above the lump, letting it flow gently over the area. Alternate this with a kaolin dressing big enough to cover the place and repeat the treatment twice a day.

Tetanus

This is very serious and can kill. It arises from infected wounds, even though the surface injury is apparently slight. As an insurance the pony should be immunized by two initial injections about a month apart, followed by a 'booster' each year (or sooner if at any time the pony sustains a severe wound).

Insect bites

Ponies, like humans, are often subject to insect bites and stings. Although these cause large alarming-looking lumps, they are usually quite soft, and will go down quickly on their own. Sometimes, however, a pony may be stung on the eyelid, near an eye or in some other very sensitive area. The discomfort can then be helped by gentle bathing with cold tea.

Don'ts

Never use any disinfectant other than salt and water or very diluted T.C.P. on a pony's skin. *Avoid* vigorous washing of any cut or wound as this can damage the surrounding tissues and so make matters worse, delaying healing.

   Never use very hot water on a pony. A pony's skin is much more sensitive than ours and it cannot stand anything as hot or as strong as we can ourselves.

Coughs

These can be serious and are usually an indication that you should call the vet. This does not mean that every time the pony gives an occasional dry cough when being ridden you must necessarily assume it is ill. It may be a sudden irritation caused by dust or pollen. Notice whether the cough persists and if it does, then take action.

A wet, thick, gurgling cough, particularly if the pony doesn't seem to be breathing normally, is a signal that you need skilled advice. If there is no cough but the pony has a runny nose, still get the vet.

Never work a pony with a cough. Remember, too, that any pony with a cough is better off in the open air than in a stable. Mollycoddling will not help. What you need is veterinary advice.

Lameness

You can probably tell when you ride it if a pony is not moving soundly. To make sure, get someone else to trot it in hand while you watch. You can then spot any irregular action.

If the pony does seem lame, examine each shoe and look under each foot for the cause of the trouble. If you can't spot anything wrong, feel for heat in the feet or legs.

Slight sprains will usually go right if the pony is kept in a field for a day or two and not worked. Trickling cold water from the garden hose over the area for twenty minutes at a time, two or three times a day will help.

A bad sprain needs the vet.

Tincture of arnica, or goose grease, are effective, inexpensive remedies that will take the soreness and ache out of a slight sprain, wrench or blow.

Injuries from a kick or blow should be dealt with as described under 'lumps'. (See also Chapter Five on Feet and Shoes.)

Laminitis

This is a kind of fever in the feet. It often arises in summer if the pony is too fat from the new grass and is then asked to do much fast trotting on the roads.

There will be heat in the feet and the pony will show signs of discomfort or lameness. The first thing to do is to call in the blacksmith to remove the pony's shoes. Then get the vet to examine the pony and advise. Skilled treatment is necessary to avoid permanent damage to the feet. Laminitis is a very serious disease which can be fatal.

Mud Fever

This can be caused by brushing in wet mud or failure to dry the legs and body properly – especially after washing – and may be treated by an application of 'white lotion' from the chemist or saddler. A bad attack may necessitate calling the vet. *Cracked heels* can also be caused by not drying the legs and inside the heels. The hollows become hot and sore. If there is a nasty discharge ('grease'), call the vet. If caught before this stage is reached, rub in vaseline or apply white lotion.

Skin troubles

Ponies occasionally get *lice*. These are tiny brown creatures which get into a pony's mane or around the base of the tail. They cause dreadful itching so that the pony scratches or rubs against trees, gates or fences until its hair is rubbed away. The vet will advise the right insecticidal treatment to remove the pests.

Ringworm is another common complaint which causes itchy bald patches that can become very red and inflamed if not treated. It is not really a worm but a fungus, and people can catch it from ponies, dogs or cattle. Similarly, a pony with ringworm can infect other animals. The treatment is simple but you need the vet to confirm. Until the trouble is cured the pony should not be ridden.

An old fashioned but effective remedy is to dab on iodine once daily. If no more patches appear after a week the pony can be reckoned free from contagion and normal grooming, riding etc, can be resumed. As ringworm is so catching, anything that has touched the pony – saddlery, grooming kit, etc, should be disinfected and put in the air and sun to dry.

Sweet Itch can sometimes be troublesome in the summer. It usually affects ponies that are unduly sensitive to midge bites. The trouble will usually disappear if the ponies are kept in their shelter during the afternoon and evening when the midges are most active. If this routine does not result in a cure, consult the vet.

Saddle sores, girth galls and sore withers

These are due to badly fitting tack. If you spot a

raised, rubbed area after a ride, bathe it with salt and water and then rub in zinc ointment or some mild antiseptic cream. Later, provided the skin is unbroken, it can be hardened with methylated spirit. Needless to say the pony should not be ridden until the place has cleared up.

Check your saddle and girth for anything that might have caused the trouble. A sheepskin pad will usually prevent it happening again. It is important to see that your saddlery fits as well as possible. (See Chapter on Tack, p. 67).

Thrush

This is a disease of the feet which usually arises from neglect. Ponies whose feet are regularly picked out and who visit the blacksmith at least every six weeks do not usually suffer from thrush. If, by mischance, your pony does get the infection you will soon know. The cleft of the frog becomes slimy and there will be an unpleasant smell when the pony's foot is picked up.

Buy a tin of Stockholm tar from the chemist or saddler. Pick out and wash the pony's feet thoroughly. Then with a short, stiff paint-brush work the Stockholm tar all over the heels, sole and frog, taking special care to get it well into the cleft and grooves. Repeat the treatment daily until the trouble clears up.

Worming

All ponies have worms and so regular treatment must be carried out at intervals of six to eight weeks.

Worm paste is the most effective and is administered by means of a syringe pushed to the back of the pony's mouth so that the mixture goes straight down the throat. With practice you will probably be able to manage this for yourself. If not, and if you have no one on hand to help who is really pony-wise, you can try using the medicine in powder-form. The pony is less likely to taste the powder and to reject it if it is placed in the refrigerator for several hours beforehand. If in doubt, ask your Pony Club Commissioner or a vet for help. Do not neglect the problem. Worm infestation can seriously affect the pony's health, being responsible for poor condition leading to colic and – in extreme cases – death.

Donkeys, which otherwise make ideal companions for ponies, are subject to a particularly dangerous form of parasite known as *lung-worm*. This can also infect ponies, so before you consider a donkey as a companion for your pony, or before you allow your pony to share a field with donkeys, have the donkey droppings checked by the vet. It takes at least three months to eradicate lung-worm infestation, so beware!

Teeth

A pony's teeth need to be checked by the vet every six months or so to see whether they need rasping. Dribbling by the bit, head-tossing, gnawing at bark or at the wood of a gate usually indicate that all is not well. Ponies' teeth wear unevenly and then they cannot chew properly, which results in loss of condition, thinness and sometimes, colic.

Nine

SAFETY FIRST

Riding is not really a dangerous sport but careless-ness and neglect can lead to nasty accidents. To prevent them it pays to observe simple precautions. The most important are outlined below.

Safety of Tack

Numerous accidents are caused by stirrup leathers that break or girths that snap. Properly cared for, tack lasts a long time. Even so, certain places in the harness are subjected to excess wear. Straps usually go at the holes. When you are cleaning tack you should always inspect these areas. Also undo all buckles before cleaning.

Stirrup leathers tend to go at the holes, especially when only one person is using them and the strain is always at the same spot. At the first sign of a break the leathers should go to the saddler, who will take them up a few inches at the buckle end. This ensures that although you are using a different hole you will still have the same length of leather.

Stirrup irons must be big enough for your foot to slip out in the event of a fall, but at the same time not so big that your foot slips right through.

Girths Whether or not you are using a nylon string girth, the leather girth straps on the saddle need watching for wear. Here you should pay par-ticular attention to the stitching of the straps at their upper end. The straps should be provided with a buckle guard to prevent the buckles chafing the saddle flap.

Bridle Here again all stitching should be frequently checked. Sweat and saliva tend to rot stiches which is why all tack should be wiped over and cleaned after use as a matter of routine.

When riding other people's ponies, whether belonging to a friend or to a riding stable, always check the tack before mounting. I have had a couple of falls due to the stirrup leathers of hired ponies breaking while on the highway.

Riding Hats Protective headgear is the most important part of a rider's safety equipment. Lack of a safety cap can lead to a fractured skull, or worse.

Even more serious is the existence of faulty, so-called 'safety' caps with inherent faults in their design which carry special hazards of their own. In one such cap the chin-strap and buckle were riveted on. In an accident one of the rivets impaled the rider's skull, unfortunately with fatal results.

B.S.I. Kite mark 6473, or British Safety Standard 4472 as specified by the Pony Club for eventing, are guarantees of efficient protection. Always look for one of these marks. The latter is based on a jockey's crash skull cap, usually velvet-covered with a leather chin cup. Alternatively you can choose a standard jockey's crash cap (jockey skull) in which jockeys ride at exercise. An effective chin cup is essential to your protection. It is important that you wear your safety hat at all times. It must be a good fit and you must wear it properly, square on your head and with the strap done up.

A new style safety cap which even exceeds BS 4472 in protecting the vulnerable areas of ears and temple, comes from Sweden and is available through saddlers. This is the Jofa which can also be obtained from Jofa UK, P/O Box 8, Petworth, Sussex. Jockey skulls on the same principle are also supplied.

Safety Tabards If you have to exercise your pony in the dusk, before or after school on winter mornings or afternoons, you should wear a luminous tabard or vest that fits loosely over your jacket and helps you to be seen more easily by other road users. Luminosity alone is not enough. The garments should be fitted with reflective strips, containing millions of tiny prisms to catch and reflect the lights of oncoming vehicles in all weathers. Reflective sashes and armbands can also be bought. Some jackets carry lettering such as 'Caution Young Rider' or 'Slow Please – Young Horse'. Your saddler will be able to show you a selection. Reflective/ fluorescent safety equipment may also be obtained from:

The British Horse Society Gift Shop, British Equestrian Centre, Stoneleigh, Kenilworth, Warwickshire CV8 2LR.

Reflectors or lights can be attached to your stirrups and your pony can be provided with a reflective tail bandage.

Boots may be of rubber or leather. Short jodphur boots or even walking shoes are all right provided they have low heels and hard, smooth soles. The heels are important to prevent your feet sliding through the stirrup and the hard soles make it easier for your feet to slip out of the irons in the event of a fall. Trainers, sandals, gym shoes, wellies, or walking shoes with ridged or studded rubber soles are out!

Road Riding Rules

Don't ride on the road after dark unless you absolutely have to.

Never ride in fog.

Don't ride in failing light or the early morning without reflective clothing and stirrup lights.

Don't ride out on the roads in snowy or icy conditions.

Never ride on the road bareback or without a properly bitted bridle.

Don't ride more than two abreast.

Never *trot* round slippery surfaces.

Don't ride in groups of three or more unless in organized ride conditions – with competent leaders and shepherds.

When riding in a group always cross the road

together. Anyone left behind might try to catch up by hurrying across when a car might be coming.

Study the appropriate sections of the Highway Code and *always* ride on the left-hand side of the road.

Always give clear and accurate signals.

Always thank or acknowledge a driver who slows down for you.

If you are leading a pony along the road always lead from your *near* (left) side. Keep yourself between the led horse and the traffic.

Road sense for ponies

You can do a great deal to familiarize your pony with the sort of frightening things it may meet when hacking out. Ponies are naturally nervous animals and it pays to remember that although they usually have good fields of vision on either side of their heads, they find difficulty in focussing clearly on things in front.

Practise riding past the family car with a door open or with the tailgate up. Stack dustbins, cartons and plastic sacks by the drive, then ride past. Get someone to rattle the dustbin lid or to sound the car horn or bang the doors as you pass. Familiarize your pony with a bicycle bell. Get someone to flap a newspaper or a sack about.

Start gently, though. You don't want your pony to bolt and cart you half way across the county. Your aim is make him steadier and traffic proof.

It helps always to speak to him calmly and pat him, or stroke his neck when he hesitates at any new experience. If he stops, however, don't give in. Use your voice to reassure him and your legs to ride him past.

There are bound to be times when your pony spooks at something on the roadside. Paper bags, torn plastic, even an odd-looking dark patch can upset a pony. When this happens his hindquarters will automatically swing out into the path of possible oncoming traffic. Your reaction will probably be to yank his head towards the roadside. Unfortunately his hindquarters will not necessarily follow. Usually they tend only to swing out further into the traffic.

As soon as your pony begins to shy, turn his head *away* from whatever he is spooking at. At the same time use your legs and riding-stick to prevent his hindquarters swinging out in the path of the traffic.

Before you take your pony on the road be sure that you can manage him with the reins in either hand. This will leave you free to stick out an arm to indicate the direction in which you intend to turn.

Teach your pony always to stand quietly and wait at road junctions, even when there is no traffic about. A pony that is in the habit of trotting on smartly as soon as he comes to a roundabout or intersection is a danger to himself and everyone on the road.

Stop, Look and Listen at every intersection. This slogan applies just as much when you are mounted as when you are on foot. In fact you should not only stop, look and listen but you should then look again, clearly signal the direction in which you intend to ride and then *look yet again* before moving off. This applies to whether you are turning left, or right, or overtaking stationary vehicles.

Listen to hear if any traffic is coming up behind you. Then turn to look behind and double check.

If the road is clear, give your signal. Then, still signalling your intention, look behind again and, if all is well, take up both reins and ride firmly and smartly across the road or round the obstruction.

Generally speaking, you are safer on than off your pony. Never dismount on the roads unless you absolutely have to. If you do, you should cross the stirrups over your saddle before dismounting so that they don't bang about and frighten the pony, then take the reins over your pony's head and keep yourself between him and the traffic.

If you are using a running martingale you cannot take the reins over the pony's head. In this case just grip them firmly about three or four inches from the pony's chin. Remember, just the same, to listen, look and signal. Then, as soon as you can, find a safe place to mount facing the direction of the oncoming traffic.

The British Horse Society runs a road safety test. If you would like to enter, tell your local Pony Club Secretary or Riding Club. There is a British Horse Society booklet *Ride and Drive Safely* that you can study in conjunction with the Highway Code. To obtain a copy write to the B.H.S. at the British Equestrian Centre, Stoneleigh, Kenilworth, Warwickshire CV8 2LR.

Tetanus

We make no apology for mentioning tetanus again. It must be taken seriously. It is a very unpleasant disease that can affect people as well as horses and ponies. It is said to be carried in horse manure and can enter the body from the soil via even the smallest scratch. Be sure to protect both yourself and your pony against this dreadful disease. Your parents will know if you have already been inoculated against tetanus. If not, get them to make arrangements with the family doctor or health centre for you to receive a jab. If you have already been inoculated check that you have had the necessary boosters. This is equally important for your pony. Keep a record of his injections and if he sustains a bad cut or gash ask the vet whether he should have an extra dose of tetanus vaccine even if he has already had his yearly booster.

Insurance

Vet's bills are expensive. Furthermore, although no one wants to think about it, ponies do occasionally suffer heart attacks, die or become so badly injured that they have to be put down. At the time you would feel that no other pony could possibly replace the one you'd lost. This is tragic but it has to be faced; time is a healer and it does help if the animal is properly covered by insurance so that you have the means to buy another.

Accidents to other people or their property can sometimes be attributed to your pony's behaviour and they could have a legal claim for damages against you. Third party insurance is vital to cover this.

Yearly insurance premiums add quite a sum to the already high cost of owning a pony but when you think of all the mishaps and illnesses that can occur it will work out cheaper in the long-run for your pony to be fully insured. The basic policy usually covers:

1. The death, or disposal of the animal on humane grounds, from any cause.

2. Public liability (claims made against you or your parents by others on the grounds that they may have suffered damage through your pony's action).

3. Theft or straying (this may include the cost of advertising the pony as missing and offering a small reward for information leading to its recovery).

In addition to this basic package you can insure against injury to yourself, your saddlery and tack and against vet's fees. Discuss the matter with your parents. Your local insurance broker, or the pony press will have details of reputable schemes.

Freeze Marking

Ask your vet, or local Pony Club about getting your pony painlessly marked with an indelible identity number so that he can readily be claimed and his ownership proved should he ever be unlucky enough to be lost or stolen.

Bear all these points in mind and I hope this book will have helped to make your pony-owning days as enjoyable and anxiety free as possible. I hope, too, it may have gone some way to making your pony as happy and comfortable as every pony deserves to be.

PONY DETAILS

Name _____

Description _____

_____

_____

_____

_____

Height in hands _____

Age of pony _____

Bought from: _____

_____

_____

_____

Stabled at: _____

_____

_____

_____

Vet's phone no. _____

Previous ailments and treatment _____

_____

_____

_____

_____

_____

_____

LIST OF TACK

_____   _____
_____   _____
_____   _____
_____   _____
_____   _____
_____   _____
_____   _____
_____   _____
_____   _____
_____   _____
_____   _____
_____   _____
_____   _____
_____   _____

PRIZES

Place	_Daté_	_Prize_
_____	_____	_____
_____	_____	_____
_____	_____	_____
_____	_____	_____
_____	_____	_____
_____	_____	_____
_____	_____	_____
_____	_____	_____
_____	_____	_____
_____	_____	_____
_____	_____	_____
_____	_____	_____
_____	_____	_____

PONY EVENTS CALENDAR

January

_____
_____
_____
_____
_____
_____
_____
_____
_____
_____

February

_____
_____
_____
_____
_____
_____
_____
_____
_____
_____

PONY EVENTS CALENDAR

March

_____
_____
_____
_____
_____
_____
_____
_____
_____
_____
_____
_____

April

_____
_____
_____
_____
_____
_____
_____
_____
_____
_____
_____
_____

PONY EVENTS CALENDAR

May

_____
_____
_____
_____
_____
_____
_____
_____
_____
_____

June

_____
_____
_____
_____
_____
_____
_____
_____
_____
_____
_____

PONY EVENTS CALENDAR

July

_____
_____
_____
_____
_____
_____
_____
_____
_____
_____
_____

August

_____
_____
_____
_____
_____
_____
_____
_____
_____
_____
_____

PONY EVENTS CALENDAR

September

_____
_____
_____
_____
_____
_____
_____
_____
_____
_____
_____

October

_____
_____
_____
_____
_____
_____
_____
_____
_____
_____
_____

PONY EVENTS CALENDAR

November

_____
_____
_____
_____
_____
_____
_____
_____
_____
_____
_____

December

_____
_____
_____
_____
_____
_____
_____
_____
_____
_____
_____
_____

NOTES

NOTES

JUDITH BERRISFORD

PIPPA'S MYSTERY HORSE

On holiday in the West Country, Pippa and her twin brother Pete have rescued a shipwrecked horse. He is a rare and valuable appaloosa – and with loving care she restores the animal to health.

Pippa knows the appaloosa should be returned to his rightful owner, but is worried by his mysterious past. The horse has been carefully trained, but also very cruelly treated. Surely not by the same person? How will she be able to find and identify the *real* owner?

KNIGHT BOOKS

JUDITH BERRISFORD

PIPPA AND THE MIDNIGHT PONIES

'Pippa! Come quickly! Hero's missing!'

Hero, a spirited black gelding, had only
been on loan to Pete for a couple of days
when he vanished. And this had happened
on the very night he and Pippa had
mounted guard on their ponies to try and
catch red-handed the mysterious nocturnal
riders.

They join forces with a group of friends in
the search for Hero and the Easter holidays
are suddenly filled with excitement,
mystery – and suspense!

KNIGHT BOOKS